Dethroning historical reputations

Universities, museums and the
commemoration of benefactors

Edited by
Jill Pellew and Lawrence Goldman

LONDON
INSTITUTE OF HISTORICAL RESEARCH

Published by

UNIVERSITY OF LONDON
SCHOOL OF ADVANCED STUDY
INSTITUTE OF HISTORICAL RESEARCH
Senate House, Malet Street, London WC1E 7HU

2018

Available to download free at http://www.humanities-digital-library.org
or to purchase at https://www.sas.ac.uk/publication/dethroning-historical-
reputations-universities-museums-and-commemoration-benefactors/

ISBN
978 1 909646 82 7 (paperback edition)
978 1 909646 83 4 (PDF edition)

DOI
10.14296/718.9781909646834

Contents

List of illustrations   v

Preface   vii

Notes on contributors   xi

1.   Introduction   1
David Cannadine

2.   Commentary on universities, museums and the
commemoration of benefactors   15
Jill Pellew

3.   The English civic universities: endowments and the
commemoration of benefactors   25
H. S. Jones

4.   Donors to an imperial project: Randlords as benefactors
to the Royal School of Mines, Imperial College of
Science and Technology   35
Jill Pellew

5.   The expectations of benefactors and a responsibility
to endow   47
John Shakeshaft

6.   The funder's perspective   57
Victoria Harrison

7.   Calibrating relevance at the Pitt Rivers Museum   65
Laura N. K. Van Broekhoven

8.   From objects of enlightenment to objects of apology:
why you can't make amends for the past by plundering
the present   81
Tiffany Jenkins

9.   British universities and Caribbean slavery   93
Nicholas Draper

10.   Risk and reputation: the London blue plaques scheme   107
Anna Eavis and Howard Spencer

11. 'A dreary record of wickedness': moral judgement in history   117
Brian Young

12. We have been here before: 'Rhodes Must Fall' in historical context   125
Lawrence Goldman

Bibliography   141

Index   145

List of illustrations

Students campaign against the decision of Oriel
College, Oxford not to remove the statue of Cecil
Rhodes from its High Street facade, 9 March 2016.   ix

Figure
4.1   Statues of Julius Wernher (L) and Alfred Beit (R),
      by Paul R Montford, erected 1910, at the entrance
      to the former Royal School of Mines, part of Imperial
      College of Science and Technology.   44
11.1 George Eliot's L.C.C. plaque of 1905 in Wimbledon
      Park Road, Wandsworth, with the wreathed border
      design. It was the first put up by the L.C.C. to a
      woman – and the first official plaque to go south of
      the River Thames.   110
11.2 Wilkie Collins was rejected for a blue plaque in 1910
      after the clerk of the L.C.C. advised that his writings
      were 'not of a high order'. His reputation having
      revived, his rectangular plaque went up in Gloucester
      Place, Marylebone, in 1951.   111
11.3 The unveiling of Ezra Pound's plaque in Kensington
      Church Walk took place in 2004.   113
12.1 Statue of Edward Colston by the sculptor Edward
      Cassidy, erected in The Centre, Bristol, in 1895, and
      the 'unauthorised heritage' plaque affixed to its base
      which remembers the millions of victims of the
      Atlantic slave trade.   133
12.2 Statue of Oliver Cromwell outside the house of
      commons, Westminster, designed by Hamo
      Thornycroft and erected in 1899.   138

Preface

Early in 2016 it seemed timely for the Institute of Historical Research to engage with the public discussion of fundamental issues connected with the history of universities and the commemoration of their benefactors. Part of the Institute's remit is to examine the historical context of activities that are key to the functioning of modern society; and specific historical issues relating to the wealth of past university benefactors have been increasingly in the forefront of public debate.

The immediate imperative was the recent 'Rhodes Must Fall' movement at Oxford. In addition, historians were becoming increasingly aware of deep concerns on certain American campuses about the source of much of their early wealth. In the case of Cecil Rhodes, a substantial benefactor to Oriel College, Oxford, objections to his racist views and his driving imperialism, led to demands for the toppling of his statue (as had been successfully achieved at Cape Town University). In the United States, universities (including Brown, Rhode Island and Georgetown, Washington, D.C.) were investigating their institutions' past benefits from slavery with a view to making restitution to descendants of those who suffered. These debates raised broad historical issues about the relationship of the present to the past.

The resulting conference, taking place at the I.H.R. over two days in March 2017, was aimed at historians of universities and institutions that have depended on benefaction; those involved in fundraising for universities; curators of museums which face their own legacy issues and many of which are departments of universities; and others involved in visible aspects of commemoration. The event was entitled 'History, Heritage and Ideology: universities and the commemoration of benefactors'.

The conference opened on the evening of 23 March with a lecture in the Chancellor's Hall, University of London, Senate House by Professor Sir David Cannadine, distinguished historian not least of philanthropy and benefaction. His title was 'Disinterested philanthropy or tainted gifts: how should historians respond to past legacies from benefactors with different social and moral values?'.

The following day discussion was focused in four sessions. First, the changing nature of benefactions to English universities and their commemoration over several centuries; second, the possible conflicts of interest between an institution's duty to uphold its reputation and its duty towards its benefactors; third, problems arising for museums through the origins of collections and their display; and fourth, broader historical issues for historians viewing the past from the perspective of the present. Each session, chaired by a facilitator, had three or four panelists as speakers to introduce discussion that was then thrown open to audience participants.

Our thanks go to our speakers: Professor Richard Rex, University of Cambridge; Professor Stuart Jones, University of Manchester; John Shakeshaft, Cambridge University Council; Victoria Harrison, former chief executive of the Wolfson Foundation; Bill Abraham, director of development, University of London; Professor William Whyte, University of Oxford; Dr. Laura Van Broekhoven, Pitt Rivers Museum, Oxford; Dr. Tiffany Jenkins, sociologist and cultural commentator; Dr. Nicholas Draper, Centre for the Study of Legacies of British Slave-ownership, University College London; and Professor Brian Young, University of Oxford. Thanks also go to the facilitators of these sessions: Daniel Snowman, I.H.R. senior research fellow and Kathrin Pieren, Jewish Museum, London. Finally, we would like to thank our I.H.R. support team, in particular, Gemma Dormer.

This publication includes contributions from the great majority of our participants to whom we are particularly grateful for their time spent transforming their speaking notes into articles.

Professor Lawrence Goldman, former director, I.H.R.
Dr. Jill Pellew, senior research fellow, I.H.R.
July 2018

Students campaign against the decision of Oriel College, Oxford not to remove the statue of Cecil Rhodes from its High Street facade, 9 March 2016.

Photograph: Chris Ratcliffe © Getty Images

Notes on contributors

DAVID CANNADINE is Dodge Professor of History at Princeton University, visiting professor at the University of Oxford, editor of the *Oxford Dictionary of National Biography* and president of the British Academy. He is author of many books, including *The Decline and Fall of the British Aristocracy, Class in Britain, Ornamentalism, Mellon* and *The Undivided Past*. His most recent book is *Victorious Century: the United Kingdom 1800–1906*.

NICHOLAS DRAPER is director of the Centre for the Study of the Legacies of British Slave-Ownership at University College London, the author of *The Price of Emancipation* (Cambridge, 2010) and co-author, with Catherine Hall and others of *Legacies of British Slave-Ownership* (Cambridge, 2014).

ANNA EAVIS is curatorial director at English Heritage, with responsibility for the presentation and conservation of over 400 historic sites and their collections. She is also responsible for London's blue plaques scheme. Having joined English Heritage in 1999 she has served on the Senior Management Team in her current capacity since 2012.

LAWRENCE GOLDMAN is professor of history at the Institute of Historical Research, University of London, and a senior research fellow of St. Peter's College, Oxford. For ten years, from its publication in 2004, he was editor of the *Oxford Dictionary of National Biography*. From 2014 to 2017 he was director of the Institute of Historical Research.

VICTORIA HARRISON was the chief executive of the Wolfson Foundation (1997–2006) after twenty-five years in the public sector (the British research councils and the Cabinet Office). Since then she has held various trusteeships of both endowed and fundraising charities, including serving as chairman of the University College London Hospitals Charity.

TIFFANY JENKINS is a sociologist, writer and broadcaster. She is an honorary fellow in the department of law at the London School of Economics and author of *Keeping their Marbles: How the Treasures of the Past Ended Up in Museums and Why They Should Stay There* (Oxford, 2016). She has also published *Contesting Human Remains in Museum Collections: the Crisis of Cultural Authority* (2014), and is the editor of *Political Culture: Soft Interventions and Nation Building* (2014).

H. STUART JONES is professor of intellectual history at the University of Manchester. His interests encompass the history of political thought, the history of the humanities and social sciences, and the history of universities, with a particular focus on nineteenth-century Britain and France. His books include *Intellect and Character in Victorian England: Mark Pattison and the Invention of the Don* (Cambridge, 2007).

JILL PELLEW is a historian of British public institutions and author of *The Home Office 1848–1914: from clerks to bureaucrats* (1982). From 1994–9 she was director of the University of Oxford's development office. Since 2009 she has been a senior research fellow at the Institute of Historical Research, University of London, and is currently working on the history of British universities and their benefactors in the nineteenth and twentieth centuries.

JOHN SHAKESHAFT is deputy chair of the Council of Cambridge University and chair of the vice-chancellor's advisory committee on benefactions and external legal engagements. He is also a board member and audit chair of Kinnevik, A.B., and investment director of Corestone, A.G. He formerly served in Her Majesty's Diplomatic Service before becoming a banker. He was educated at Cambridge, Princeton and S.O.A.S.

HOWARD SPENCER is a senior historian at English Heritage and has worked on the London blue plaques scheme for the last thirteen years. Previously he was a research editor at the *Oxford Dictionary of National Biography* and a research fellow at the History of Parliament. He has also worked as a local newspaper editor and as a media relations consultant. He is editor of *The English Heritage Guide to London's Blue Plaques*.

LAURA VAN BROEKHOVEN is director of the Pitt Rivers Museum, University of Oxford. Previously she led the curatorial department of the National Museum of World Cultures (Amsterdam, Leiden and Berg en Dal) and was a lecturer in archaeology, museum studies and indigenous heritage at Leiden University. She has published widely in her specialist subject, central and south American archaeology and ethnography. Current museological interests include repatriation and redress, with a focus on the importance of collaboration, inclusivity and open-minded enquiry.

BRIAN YOUNG is a University Lecturer in history at Oxford, where he is the Charles Stuart Tutor at Christ Church. He is the author of *Religion and Enlightenment in Eighteenth-Century England* (Oxford, 1998) and of *The Victorian Eighteenth Century* (Oxford, 2007). He is currently completing a study of relations between Christians and unbelievers in eighteenth-century England, and has written widely on intellectual and religious history.

1. Introduction

David Cannadine

Once a year, and sometimes more often, many Oxford and Cambridge colleges engage in rituals that are collectively known as the 'commemoration of benefactors'. They are attended by distinguished guests, honorary fellows and fellows, and sometimes by graduate students and undergraduates, and they often involve a grand dinner with splendid food and abundant wine. Such feasts are normally preceded by a service held in the college chapel, when a sermon is preached, saluting the venerable largesse of earlier donors, and when their names are read out in what is often a lengthy recitation, which frequently concludes with an appropriately uplifting peroration:

> These are our founders and principal benefactors, whose names we have thus publicly recited, to the service and glory of God, to the perpetuating of their memory, and to the demonstration of our gratitude.

Such occasions are also designed to reaffirm the historic continuity of college life, and the sustaining appeal of institutional identity, and they can be genuinely moving, as I can well attest, having myself attended several such gatherings in Oxford and Cambridge, and on one occasion even preaching the obligatory sermon. Yet it is not necessary to be an anthropologist to recognize that such ceremonies and commemorations are also classic examples of what might be termed institutionalized ancestor worship.

These ritual observances and celebrations of benefactors are particularly identified with Oxford and Cambridge colleges, but individual giving has been important, indeed essential, across most of British higher education for most of its history. This has certainly been true of the Scottish universities, of the constituent colleges which make up the University of London, and of the great civic redbricks of Liverpool, Leeds, Manchester, Sheffield, Birmingham and Bristol, all of which relied on private philanthropy (as well as student fees) long before the British state committed itself to the large-scale funding of higher education in the aftermath of the Second World War. Where would the University of Oxford be without the founding gift of Sir Thomas Bodley, which established what would eventually become one of the great libraries of the world? Where would the University of Cambridge be, without the Fitzwilliam Museum and the Cavendish Laboratory, both the

D. Cannadine, 'Introduction', in *Dethroning historical reputations: universities, museums and the commemoration of benefactors*, ed. J. Pellew and L. Goldman (2018), pp. 1–13.

products of (unusual and atypical) aristocratic generosity in the nineteenth century? Where would the University of Birmingham be without the major gift that Joseph Chamberlain successfully secured from Andrew Carnegie, or the University of Bristol without the support of the Wills family? Where, in the University of London, would the Warburg Institute be, without the benevolence of its eponymous founders? And where would the Institute of Historical Research be without the initial benefaction of £20,000 that Professor A. F. Pollard obtained in 1921 from Sir John Cecil Power?

I

It is, then, beyond doubt that the connection between private philanthropy and higher education in the United Kingdom has been both long lived and in many ways beneficent and benign; and it is, for obvious reasons, a connection which is of much longer-standing than in the case of the great, but less venerable, universities of the United States. Yet apart from the annual commemorations in Oxbridge colleges, it is a philanthropic history that was largely forgotten on this side of the Atlantic during the years from 1945 to the 1970s, when higher education became increasingly dependent on funding from the British state, as exemplified by the government-sponsored foundation of new universities in the 1960s (endorsed by the Robbins Report of 1963), and when the unprecedentedly successful efforts at fundraising that were by then being undertaken by American universities from rich alumni and foundations were often disparaged in this country for being vulgar and inappropriate (and, in the British case, unnecessary). Only since the 1980s have universities in the United Kingdom begun to engage with what is now termed 'development' in the sort of serious, systematic and aggressive way that has for much longer been characteristic of their American counterparts: employing fundraising staff, mounting public appeals, targeting their own alumni, and seeking major donors and cultivating potential prospects from rich individuals and foundations, not only in the United Kingdom and the United States, but increasingly in Asia and Australia. Indeed, as any head of an Oxbridge college or university chancellor or vice-chancellor well knows, raising money and schmoozing possible donors are now essential and time-consuming parts of their job, involving extensive wining and dining and much foreign travel.

In recent decades, and on both sides of the Atlantic, university fundraising has become more widespread, more important, more professionalized and more competitive than ever before. Perhaps this in turn helps explain why such activities have also become more controversial and, in some famous instances, fraught with grave reputational risk to particular universities, which have suffered serious embarrassment as a result of fundraising efforts that were ill-judged and went badly wrong. Here is one example. In 1995, Yale University returned a gift of $20 million to the Texan billionaire and alumnus Lee Bass, on the grounds that the donor's demand to have veto powers over faculty appointments to teach the courses in western civilization that his gift was intended to fund, would constitute unacceptable interference in the University's academic freedom and autonomy. And here is another. In 2008, Princeton University settled a six-year lawsuit brought by the Robertson family, who contended that the $35 million benefaction made by Charles Robertson in 1961 to establish the Woodrow Wilson School of Public Affairs had not been spent in accordance with the terms of the original gift, and they wanted their money back. In the end, Princeton kept the money, but the University also agreed to pay out millions of dollars to defray the Robertson family's legal fees.

As these two examples suggest, the giving or receiving of gifts in the world of higher education can result in both parties being dissatisfied and disillusioned: universities may be unhappy with what donors want, and donors may be unhappy with what universities do, and there have been similar, recent episodes in the United Kingdom as well as in the United States. In 1996, Dr. Gert-Rudolph Flick gave the University of Oxford £360,000 over five years to endow the appropriately named Flick Professorship of European Political Thought. But it soon emerged that Flick's grandfather had built the industrial empire which was the basis of the family fortune while serving as an adviser to Heinrich Himmler, and there was widespread criticism of Oxford for having accepted what was deemed to have been such a tainted gift. Having made his donation in good faith, Dr. Flick was mortified by these public attacks, and asked for his money back; Oxford duly returned it, and Flick's name was no longer associated with the chair. Instead, it was supported by an anonymous donor, who specifically wanted to support intra-European academic co-operation. And in 2011, Sir Howard Davies felt obliged to resign as the director of the London School of Economics, when it was revealed that the L.S.E. had accepted a donation of £300,000 to support work on civil society in North Africa from the Gaddafi International Charity and Development Corporation, which was run by the son of the Libyan dictator, Colonel Gaddafi, who was himself an L.S.E. graduate. The subsequent inquiry chaired by Lord Woolf concluded that the School's vetting procedures for assessing potential donors had been inadequate, and as a result they have been significantly tightened up.

More recently, there have been the campaigns against Cecil Rhodes in Oxford, and against Woodrow Wilson at Princeton, where undergraduates have urged that their universities should no longer commemorate past benefactors or leaders whose conduct and opinions (especially on matters of race) now seem at best inappropriate, at worst offensive, judged by our own very different ethical standards, and in the (often outraged) opinion of those who belong to a much more diverse student body, of which African-Americans form a significant proportion. As a result of these controversies (and they are far from being the only ones), universities on both sides of the Atlantic, and many other cultural institutions which also depend on fundraising to support their programs, acquisitions and building plans, have been falling over themselves to establish ethics committees. They in turn have been charged with setting out general guidelines concerning the acceptance of gifts, and they have also been tasked with assessing and evaluating potential donations in the light of them. All this is a long way from the eloquent cadences quoted near the beginning of this introduction, and the easy certainties they expressed, which now seem almost pitifully naïve. Far from being simple, straightforward, honourable, high-minded and transactionally symmetrical – admired donor generously gives, enhanced institution gratefully receives, and ancestor worship subsequently ensues – philanthropy nowadays can often seem an enterprise fraught with moral ambiguity, likely to provoke student protest and running the risk of damaging publicity.

It was, then, both timely and appropriate that the Institute of Historical Research should have sponsored a conference in the spring of 2017 that was devoted to exploring these controversies and these issues, and I was greatly honoured to be invited to offer some general thoughts and reflections to frame the proceedings. I did so, not only as a former director of the I.H.R., but also as an academic with experience of both British and American higher education, and as a historian of philanthropy, who has been responsible for raising money, and for helping to give money away. One of my books is a biography of Andrew Mellon, the Pittsburgh banker and plutocrat, who donated a large part of his fortune, and all his finest pictures, to establish the National Gallery of Art in Washington, D.C.; and my current major research project is to write the history of the Ford Foundation, which for much of the second half of the twentieth century was both the largest and the most controversial philanthropist in the United States. Since the late 1990s, I have also been active in raising money, primarily for the Institute of Historical Research and now for the British Academy, but also for the National Portrait Gallery, the Royal Academy, the National Trust and the Gladstone Library. From yet a third perspective, I have become, albeit indirectly, a philanthropic practitioner, as a trustee of the Wolfson Foundation, which is much involved in supporting higher education, and whose Arts Panel I chair. It is from these varied viewpoints that I look at past philanthropy in the light of current ethical concerns, and offer some speculative comments on present and future giving.

II

How, then, should we now deal with past philanthropists and their benefactions, and with their resulting institutional commemoration and celebration, when certain individuals now seem far less admirable than they once did, when their gifts appear tainted rather than talismanic, and when their values and attitudes seem not just different from our own, but at best unacceptable, and at worst abhorrent and deplorable? The classic case of this is the recent 'Rhodes Must Fall' campaign, which began in South Africa, at the University of Cape Town, and subsequently took off in Oxford. The University of Cape Town is housed on land that was donated by the Rhodes estate, and a statue to him was unveiled on the campus in 1932; but it was removed in April 2015 in response to widespread undergraduate protests, especially by African students who were offended by its continuing presence. For more than one hundred years, the University of Oxford has awarded Rhodes scholarships to promising young men (and more recently women) from the British Empire (now Commonwealth), the United States and Germany (intermittently). There is a (much smaller) statue commemorating Rhodes in a niche high up on the Oxford High Street façade of Oriel, his own college; and Rhodes House is the headquarters of the scholarships that bear his name. By the standards of its time, and still in real terms today, Rhodes's gift was a prodigiously generous benefaction, and from a man once widely esteemed as a great British patriot and empire builder. Yet today, by contrast, Cecil Rhodes stands condemned by many people as a racist and as an imperialist, and as being no longer deserving of Oxford University's approbation and commemoration.

In more detail, the case against Rhodes is as follows: he made a fortune in gold and diamonds, exploiting black labourers working down the mines in ways that would be unacceptable today. The British South Africa Company, of which he was the founder and chief shareholder, was a rapacious exemplar of capitalism and imperialism at their worst, its treatment of King Lobenguala of the Matabele was beyond deplorable, and the loose morals and mores of the Company's employees, in administering Rhodesia and Nyasaland, were unacceptable even by the lax standards of the late nineteenth century, let alone today. Moreover, Rhodes was complicit – and was proven at the time to have been complicit – in the Jameson Raid, launched in December 1895 as an unlawful attempt to overthrow the Transvaal government which, whatever its faults, was the legitimately elected authority of an independent sovereign state. And in observing that 'the British are the finest race in the world, and the more of the world they inhabit, the better it will be for mankind', Rhodes might have said something that was the conventional wisdom to Anglo-Saxons in 1900, but a century further on, such imperialist arrogance and racist bigotry is no longer deemed acceptable, and least of all in Oxford, where one aspect of the University's mission is to encourage ethnic diversity among undergraduates.

The 'Rhodes Must Fall' movement is only one example of protests that have taken place on university campuses on both sides of the Atlantic. Yale University has recently agreed that Calhoun College will be renamed, on the grounds that John C. Calhoun was one of the last high-profile defenders of slavery in the United States during the first half of the nineteenth century, and that it is no longer right to commemorate and venerate such a racist and reprehensible figure on a campus with a significant African-American population. Instead, the college has been renamed for Grace Brewster Murray Hopper, a woman, an admiral in the U.S. Navy, a computer scientist and a Yale graduate student. Yale has also agreed that it will no longer call the heads of its colleges 'Masters', on the grounds that the association of this word with the superiorities and inferiorities of slavery is again both reprehensible and inappropriate in a university with an ethnically diverse student body. There have also been student protests at Princeton University against what was deemed to be the sanitized veneration of Woodrow Wilson, embodied in the naming of Wilson College and the Woodrow Wilson School of Public Affairs, on the grounds that Wilson was a southern racist, and that whatever may have been his achievements as governor of New Jersey and president of the United States, he should not be held up to acclaim in the university of which he was once president, on the grounds that Princeton now espouses very different (and more enlightened) values from those which he proclaimed. Like Rhodes and like Calhoun, so this argument runs, Wilson is an ancestor who should no longer be worshipped.

Hence in Oxford, the demand that, as in the University of Cape Town, the statue of Rhodes must be removed, on the grounds that its continued presence is both offensive and provocative, especially to undergraduates of colour. For if, so this argument runs, the University of Oxford is genuine in its claim that it stands today for equality of access, for the ending of racism and racial prejudice, and for a world-view that extends beyond British or Eurocentric parochialism, then the continued celebration of Rhodes, who seems the very antithesis of the values that Oxford now embraces, must end. Hence the additional demands that the money Rhodes left to Oriel should be repaid, that the Rhodes scholarships should be both renamed and rethought, and that the Oxford history syllabus should be 'de-colonialized'. But that is not the only view that has been taken of this matter. One alternative position concedes that Rhodes is not a figure who would command contemporary approbation, but also insists that he was undeniably a significant historical personage and a no-less significant

Oxford benefactor. Yet we also need to recognize, so this argument goes, that Rhodes was a figure of his time, with the prejudices and presuppositions of his time, who needs to be understood and judged by the standards of his time. Context is all, and contexts change, and the context has certainly changed in Rhodes's case. That being so, this argument continues, we should not seek to obliterate Rhodes from the historical record, by pulling down his statue, or by renaming Rhodes House. Instead, we should explain that Rhodes's time was not our time; but we should also recognize his historical and philanthropic importance, even if his values were not as ours.

In the case of Woodrow Wilson, there have been similar demands in Princeton to those made in Cape Town and Oxford about Rhodes or at Yale about Calhoun: that his name should be removed from Wilson College, and from the Woodrow Wilson School, since it is a reproach and an insult to African-American Princeton students, and should be replaced by that of someone else more acceptable to, and exemplary of, contemporary values and sensibilities. No such changes have yet been made, but Princeton did set up a working party to look more fully into Wilson's views and achievements than the University had been willing to countenance before, and it has published the findings of the wide variety of historians whom it consulted. The result has been a broad recognition that Wilson did, indeed, hold views on the subject of race that seem unacceptable to us now, and that whatever his national achievements as an educator and his international accomplishments as American president, these less admirable aspects of his life need to be recognized. One response is that his views, while reprehensible now, were no worse than those which were generally held in his day, and that it is ahistorical and anachronistic to condemn someone by the later standards of our different era. Another is to insist that even by the standards of his own time, Wilson's segregationist and racist attitudes were indeed reprehensible. Yet a third is that, notwithstanding his shortcomings, Wilson was a major figure in the history of Princeton, of his country and of the wider world, and should be treated as such, but no longer be regarded as a fit subject for ancestor worship.

So far, the official responses of Oxford concerning Rhodes, Yale on Calhoun, and Princeton in regard to Wilson have been different; but all three universities have been forced to recognize that previously acclaimed and venerated figures can no longer be viewed in an uncritical light, and that something must be done, ranging from the removal of Calhoun's name at Yale, via deeper historicization in the case of Wilson at Princeton, to a recognition that multicultural and postcolonial Oxford has to do better, although in ways not yet fully worked out, and even if Rhodes's statue remains (at least for now). But, as invariably in these cases, these are not the only views. One alternative is to argue that it is misguided and in fact impossible to set out to atone for what are now deemed the 'wrongs' of the past, because the past is indeed and by definition a foreign country, and that they did do things differently there. Nor, so this argument continues, is it right to obliterate from the past, and to expunge from the historical record, those events, people and reputations that we now deem unpleasant and unacceptable. That may be what Communist countries and African dictatorships do, especially when their ruling regimes change, but it is not what the freedom-loving west should do. On the contrary, and as Eric Hobsbawm once remarked, the historian's job is to be 'the professional remembrancers of what their fellow citizens wish to forget'.

It was, after all, none other than Edward Gibbon who, several centuries ago, urged that history was little more than the record of the crimes, follies and misfortunes of mankind. So it is hardly a novel insight to be told that there is much in the past, in terms of people, events and reputations, which many nowadays find distasteful. The past is not a place for the squeamish, you cannot hug your way through history, and it is a mistaken idea to try. But in modification and extension of Gibbon's dictum, we also need to recognize that what are retrospectively deemed to have been mankind's crimes, follies and misfortunes do change over time, and they have especially changed during the last half century. As John Vincent once provocatively observed, we in the west now live in societies that are, or at least generally aspire to be, liberal, secular, democratic, feminist and egalitarian. But from such perspectives, this means that most of the human past was not like that and is not like that. Accordingly, the most important task for university educators, so this argument continues, should not be to give in to demands to produce a sanitized and bowdlerized version of the past, expunging from it those many people and events that now seem offensive to today's values and sensibilities: on the contrary, our prime task, in helping undergraduates on their way to adulthood, should be (among other things) to try to get them to understand how keenly, honestly and painfully people in earlier times held views, pursued aims, entertained opinions and did things, that now seem to us wrong, misguided and even abhorrent.

Moreover, it is not only the past that was a sinful place and an imperfect world, inhabited by sinful and imperfect people, for the same is true of the present (and it will no doubt be true of the future as well); and among those past and present sinners are indeed to be found many entrepreneurs, industrialists, businesspeople, bankers, philanthropists, university leaders, politicians and United States presidents. Part of our job as educators is to confront these uncomfortable but undeniable truths ourselves, and also to ensure that the undergraduates we teach will have done so, too, for how else are we to discharge another of our tasks, namely that of preparing them for life in the flawed, fallible and sinful world that they themselves are going to inhabit? And in the process of doing so, we should not be obliterating figures such as Calhoun, Wilson and Rhodes from the historical record because some or most of what they did causes pain and offence to us, here, now, today. On the contrary, we should be explaining how and why they thought and did what they did and when they did; we should recognize that with all their faults (as it now seems to us), they were undeniably major historical figures of their time; and, in the case of Rhodes, we might at least be willing to concede that what we now regard as his ill-gotten gains have nevertheless been put to good use in the years since his death. Indeed, there are many past examples of tainted money that was eventually given away for admirable purposes. But what should be the attitudes of universities today, in the light of these recent controversies, if they are confronted with offers of what are now be deemed to be corrupted and contaminated giving?

III

Before getting to that question, it is important to state what is surely an obvious and incontrovertible point, that is equally valid on both sides of the Atlantic, namely that for the foreseeable future, as the costs of higher education continue to rise, the need for fundraising and the pursuit of philanthropic largesse is going to become more important to universities, not less. (The continuing digital revolution may at some distant date mean that all higher education will be provided and undertaken online, and that many campus-based universities, with full-time faculty and resident students will become a thing of the past; but despite the proliferation of M.O.O.C.s, that doesn't seem likely to be happening any time soon.) In the United States and the United Kingdom, the respective consequences of the Trump presidency and the Brexit vote may well mean that less government money will be available for universities. On both sides of the Atlantic, there are also real and pressing problems with raising tuition fees further: in America because they are already deemed to be far too high at top-tier universities and colleges; in Britain because to do so would be politically very controversial, and it seems likely that fees may soon be reduced. And given the widespread recognition that universities are stronger if their sources of income are correspondingly varied, then the search for big, philanthropic money is going to intensify rather than diminish.

Yet it bears repeating that at the very same time that philanthropic income is becoming of ever greater significance in the world of higher education, the pursuit of such benefactions is becoming increasingly challenging: partly because in today's anxious and competitive climate, more universities are aggressively pursuing what is in reality a finite number of major donors, both actual and potential; and partly because there is a growing divergence between the need to raise big sums from such sources, and the recognition that such funding may be deemed to be morally unacceptable, however financially welcome it might be – or would be. Some years ago, a major figure in the cultural world of London told me that the most important point to bear in mind, when it came to fundraising, was not so much where the money came from or how it had originally been made, but what good you could do with it if and when you got it. There is abundant historical evidence that this view has often been taken in the past, but is it sustainable or justifiable now? Would, for example, the University of Oxford today accept another monster and potentially transformative benefaction from a figure as controversial as we now regard Cecil Rhodes as having been? It seems highly unlikely, and maybe Oxford would be right to turn it down. Yet the Rhodes scholarships have undoubtedly changed the lives of many people from many parts of the world for the better, and this has often been to considerable public benefit, and greatly to Oxford's benefit as well.

The fact that bad money can be put to good use means that this is far from being a wholly straightforward issue, and when it comes to fundraising today, it is not the only one. Here is another. On both sides of the Atlantic, universities repeatedly proclaim their commitment to equality, diversity, cosmopolitanism, internationalism, the pursuit of truth, the significance of evidence-based learning, and the importance of freedom of thought. These are undoubtedly admirable attitudes and attributes, especially in the strident, populist era of Brexit Britain and Trump's America, where 'fake news' and xenophobia seem ominously on the rise. But today, as in the past, many rich people have inherited fortunes that were ill-gotten gains, or have made their own money by means that will not survive ethical scrutiny, and many more of them may not share the attitudes and beliefs enumerated earlier in this paragraph. Yet they are wealthy, and some of them are potentially generous – perhaps motivated by the wish for social acceptance, or by a genuine desire to do good (or to atone?) by giving money away. But they would be highly unlikely to pass the stringent tests of the ethics committees which most universities now have in place to evaluate the moral credentials of potential donors, in the hope of avoiding precisely the sort of difficulties and the negative publicity that Yale and Princeton, and Oxford and the L.S.E., have recently encountered.

Moreover, from a philanthropic perspective, it is not only those who seek to raise money who nowadays are more than ever concerned with ethical issues. For just as universities are increasingly eager to proclaim that they have an ethical acceptance policy, so many foundations, which exist to give money away, are equally keen to proclaim that they have an ethical investment policy. Some such bodies will no longer invest in companies concerned with (for example) armaments, fossil fuel, tobacco or gambling; while many universities will not accept money that comes from what are deemed to be such tainted sources. These are in many ways admirable positions to take up, and the pressure for those foundations and universities that have not yet adopted such ethical codes seems unrelenting (especially from undergraduates in the case of fossil fuels). But good intentions may not necessarily yield good results or the right results. On the one hand, the investment portfolios of many rich institutions (and individuals) are managed by so many different people at so many varied levels, and the world of global capitalism is so complex and multifarious in its many interconnections, that in reality such high-minded restrictions can be very hard to maintain, enforce and police. On the other hand, if universities make their ethical requirements too stringent and exacting, they may significantly limit and hamper their capacity to raise substantial sums of money, because potential donors will not be willing to subject themselves to such moral monitoring.

In the long history of university funding in Britain, this is in many ways an unprecedented state of affairs: where the need for philanthropic largesse and support for higher education has never been greater, but where anxieties over the sources and motivations of such funding on the part of universities have never been greater, either. And, given that some dubious donors undoubtedly seek to gain respectability or influence by such means, these concerns are not wholly unreasonable. This in turn means that universities seeking philanthropic funding increasingly find themselves in a position that is at once high-minded but restricting, as they attempt to obtain more money from foundations and rich individuals, even as they also wish, via their recently established ethics committees, to sit in judgement on the very philanthropies and the very people whose largesse they seek to secure in unprecedented amounts. For any development office, tasked with raising more money than ever before, this is a very difficult position in which to be put: trying to attract and engage potential donors, while in the process also warning them that their business and investment practices may be subject to rigorous investigation, as a result of which any impending benefaction may be refused for fear of offending ethical guidelines (and/or undergraduate opinion).

How many potential donors, eager to do altruistic good, or to acquire respectability and social recognition, or to atone for earlier misdoings and misdeeds, or for whatever other motives, will in future be willing to submit themselves to such increased scrutiny, from the very organization to which they wish to give, thereby running the risk of being rebuffed, humiliated, and losing face and reputation? Moreover, in philanthropy, as in so much else in life, what is sauce for the goose is sauce for the gander. For if would-be donors are willing to persevere, and if their gifts are eventually accepted, then it will be scarcely surprising if enhanced vigilance and concern on the part of those seeking gifts is paralleled by increased determination on the part of those who give for much more rigorous impact assessments, and a growing insistence on the meeting of agreed performance targets, than has generally been the case in the past. No individual or institution is likely to submit themselves to the sort of rigorous ethical vetting that is becoming the norm without in turn imposing their own increasingly stringent requirements on those to whom they have eventually been allowed to give their money. At just the time when there is a greater need than ever before for philanthropic support for higher education, those seeking such gifts, and those who might be minded to make them, are both becoming more demanding and hard-nosed in their negotiations and in the processes and procedures they want to see followed. Will there be more philanthropy or less as a result? Will fundraising get easier or become more difficult? Only time will tell.

One final point. According to Owen Chadwick, one of the prime purposes of studying history has always been to free us from what he called 'the tyranny of present-day opinion'. For it is the besetting weakness of every generation to presuppose that it is the wisest, the most sophisticated, the most moral and the most high-minded of any that has ever lived, and that all of history had been leading up to this most admirable state of affairs. But what history actually shows, to the contrary, is that there is no parochialism as easy or as pervasive as the temporal parochialism of the present. Like many generations that have gone before, we may think ourselves superior to our forebears, which helps explain why some people are hostile to previous philanthropies based on very different and less admirable values; but that being so, should we not at least entertain the possibility that future generations may take an equivalently disapproving view of us? This might, in turn, suggest that it is unwise to draw up ethical guidelines regarding potential donors that are too precise, and too difficult to change. No doubt universities need some essential basic criteria for determining whether potential gifts are acceptable or not; but they will also need to be flexible, as circumstances and values and student opinion continue to develop and to evolve. Here is one potential straw in the wind. Undergraduate hostility to fossil fuels is also accompanied by an increasing preference for vegetarian meals. Might this mean that at some future date, universities will be ill-advised to accept money from foundations associated with the sale of meat, poultry and game, or from individuals who like their filet mignon or their beef wellington, and enjoy hunting and shooting? Once again, only time will tell ...

IV

All of this is but another way of saying that, like many other facets of human existence and experience, philanthropic practices and fundraising endeavours are simultaneously timeless yet also time-bound. They extend at least as far back in history to the three wise men presenting their Christmas gifts to the baby Jesus in the stable at Bethlehem; yet they also take particular forms at specific times which in our own day are in significant ways different from earlier practices, and which are becoming even and ever more so. From one perspective, philanthropy has never been more necessary or important to the work, health and future of higher education than it is now; from another angle, giving away money to universities has never been an activity more controversial or more fraught with risk than it is now; and from yet a third vantage point, there has never been a greater demand, or a greater need, for rules and guidelines for the giving and the receiving of grants and benefactions than there is now. Against this challenging and changing background, the essays that follow seek to offer new historical perspectives on philanthropy and fundraising in British universities and other cultural institutions, to explore and examine some famous and controversial instances of giving and getting, and to describe some recent attempts to engage with contemporary ethical concerns. They make for salutary and stimulating reading.

2. Commentary on universities, museums and the commemoration of benefactors

Jill Pellew

The commemoration of major donors to universities over the centuries has taken various forms. Sometimes the names of institutions themselves have preserved the memory of these donors, such as John Moores University, Liverpool, or the Bodleian Library, Oxford. The proverbial 'man on the street' may know nothing about John Moores or Thomas Bodley but thus knows their names as an institutional and geographical location. Sometimes, when donors are commemorated by statues – such as those of Lady Margaret Beaufort, high over the entrance to St. John's College, Cambridge and the now notorious Cecil Rhodes at Oriel College, Oxford – these may evoke greater interest from the visually inclined. Every so often, one of those men on the street might enquire about those names and those statues, become intrigued and ask why their names and images are attached to a great library, to ancient colleges or to a university. Such historical inquiry, followed by rational discussion, is an important aspect of a cultured society.

How, therefore, should historians react to a relatively new phenomenon, the movement to change the name of an institution or to pull down commemorative statues when these are found offensive to interest groups whose members may be descendants of those who were exploited by the individuals being celebrated and who regard such actions as an appropriate means of making reparations for actions and *mores* of a bygone era with very different ethical values? The practice of obliterating the name and memory of an individual – particularly one who was not only a significant benefactor but also a lauded figure in his/her lifetime – raises further fundamental issues for historians who work to understand the past and to convey it to the present. Denial of the past through obliteration of evidence is a serious impediment to historical understanding. Are there not other, more positive ways in which those who live now can demonstrate that they have different value systems from those of their forebears? From the point of view of a historian, does this not include his/her commitment to ascertain and set out the broad context of their subjects' lives, customs, beliefs and motivation?

J. Pellew, 'Commentary on universities, museums and the commemoration of benefactors', in *Dethroning historical reputations: universities, museums and the commemoration of benefactors*, ed. J. Pellew and L. Goldman (2018), pp. 15–24.

Further than this, should historians not make ethical judgements about those past individuals, knowing – as Professor Cannadine has reminded us – that they too are 'men of their time' and need to be humble about the inevitable limitations of understanding of how they themselves will be judged by future generations?

These were the underlying issues of our day's four sessions examining the history and ideology of universities and museums in the commemoration of their benefactors.

English university benefactors over time: changing issues in the context of today's ethical standards

H. S. Jones, 'The English civic universities: endowments and the commemoration of benefactors'

J. Pellew, 'Donors to an imperial project: Randlords as benefactors to the Royal School of Mines, Imperial College of Science and Technology'

The story of English university benefactions has a long history, going back to the founding of colleges in Oxford and Cambridge in the thirteenth century. From then, for over seven centuries, colleges and the universities which they later became (or formed part of) depended for their foundation and development on private endowment and financial contributions. Only after the Second World War, when the concept of a British welfare state included widening opportunities in higher education, were new universities founded and funded primarily through taxation administered by central government. That era over, when a weakened economy and then a different political philosophy returned universities to a new period of a 'mixed economy', private philanthropy was to return as a significant income stream for many universities.

This is a vast time frame within which to generalize about benefactors. But, hopefully, it is possible to make meaningful comparisons by focusing on three universal aspects of major benefaction: the context within which the wealth of benefactors was acquired; the motivation that stimulated this financial support; and the long-term value of the educational project. It is beyond the scope of the present volume to examine these aspects over the broad expanse of English history; and the focus of our contributions here is on the nineteenth and early twentieth centuries. But, by way of a prelude it is important to touch on benefactors of the late medieval/early modern period in an attempt to illustrate these comparators.

The starting point for historians of benefaction and for professional fundraisers is the question: where are the great sources of wealth? The clear response for pre-Reformation England is that overwhelming wealth (and therefore power) lay with the Church, the principal inspiration in the founding of all educational institutions. Princes of the Church – both secular (bishops) and religious (abbots) – were great feudal magnates, with land, property and associated rents.[1] Among the monarch's senior advisers, they provided the administrative infrastructure of medieval power and politics. They held the moral and professional responsibility for providing different levels of education and in maintaining standards of literacy. They well understood that in much of Christendom universities were the training ground not only for those going into the Church but also for clerks in royal or baronial service. And they were not averse to promoting the interests of their wider families: a common feature of their benefactions was the provision of places in their colleges specifically for 'founder's kin'. The outstanding ecclesiastical benefactor was William of Wykeham whose foundation of New College, Oxford, set in train the founding, between 1379 and 1529, of seven major Oxford colleges by senior bishops from among the richest sees. Royalty also left collegiate legacies: Henry VI with King's, Cambridge; Lady Margaret Beaufort with St. John's and Christ's, Cambridge; and Henry VIII with his completion of what became Christ Church, Oxford. These corporate collegiate institutions were based on the monastic model. This underpinned the strong personal motives of some of the founders for whom an important aspect of their benefaction was the commitment of the institution to pray for their souls in order to ease their way through purgatory.

> Death and its aftermath were a constant preoccupation of most people, and a bad death came to a person who had not prepared. Preparation included ... an investment of time and money in good works, and the setting up of arrangements for prayers after death.[2]

In the post-Reformation period new sources of wealth, in more secular contexts, led to a broader range of college founders at Oxford and Cambridge. Men in the service of the crown, such as Sir William Petre – re-founder of Exeter College, Oxford in 1566–8 – earned good fees and perquisites from international statesmanship. Thomas White – founder of St. John's College, Oxford in 1555 – made his fortune in the City of London whence he was able to procure large-scale loans for the king. New foundations were partly inspired by broader social motives, such as a sense of obligation to provide

---

[1] The see of Winchester, whose estate included some 60 manors, brought its 14th-century incumbents an income that made them some of the richest in western Christendom.
[2] M. Rubin, *The Hollow Crown* (2005), p. 293.

educational opportunities not only for kin, but more generally for the young in a founder's locality. Yet for much of the sixteenth century issues of religion and concomitant issues of faith and piety remained to the fore. Fear of purgatory still haunted some. The re-founder of Magdalene College, Cambridge in 1542, Sir Thomas Audley, and the founder of Trinity College, Oxford in 1555, Sir Thomas Pope, had made their fortunes working in Henry VIII's court of augmentations, administering the massive transfer of land and property resulting from the dissolution of the monasteries. At a time when prices were rising, onward selling of such land was a lucrative business that enriched professional civil servants whose skills were required in the management of crown finances. These founders had effectively made their fortunes through land speculation. Moreover, Pope and Petre had lingering Catholic sympathies and might well have been impelled by a sense of Catholic guilt to found what were effectively chantries partly to pray for their souls. Certainly the statutes of the well-endowed Trinity College, Oxford show a strong leaning towards the purgatorial aspect of prayers for the founder (and his wife).[3]

Often these colleges were not called after their founder but rather reflected Christian affiliation (such as Magdalen and All Souls, Oxford; and St. Catherine's and Christ's, Cambridge). Nevertheless, they and subsequent Oxford and Cambridge benefactors were commemorated by 'their' institutions in more material ways than prayer, such as through the erection of statues and the commissioning of portraits – the 'ancestor worship' referred to by Professor Cannadine.[4]

As far as the final of our parameters for judging the value of major benefactions is concerned – the long-term value of the institutional object of benefaction – there has been little controversy. Few would deny that the creation of the universities mentioned has not been a public good.[5] If good has come out of such benefactions, should the origin of the wealth that underpinned them and the motivation of the donors in making them be censured? Furthermore, how far back do sensitivities about such matters go? Does anyone today care how benefactors to Oxford colleges, Balliol (John de Balliol) or Christ Church (Cardinal Wolsey) came by their fortunes? It does not seem so. This is partly perhaps because most humans can better relate to a past within ancestral memory. But it is more to do with what underlies today's objections to the source of particular

    [3] C. Hopkins, *Trinity: 450 Years of an Oxford College Community* (Oxford, 2005), p. 25. See also J. Pellew, 'Philanthropists who left a lasting legacy', *Oxford Today*, xx (2008), 20

    [4] See above, p. 1.

    [5] The great majority of those English universities mentioned are in today's prestigious 'Russell Group'.

wealth – the exploitation of human beings. Such objections focus less on what one might view as exploitation by northern industrialists – such as the Manchester textile producers – of vulnerable young child workers in their cotton factories than on those exploited in the production of the key element of their business, raw cotton produced by slaves across the Atlantic. For it is the outcome of British colonial-related trade and manufacture and its strong element of sometimes brutal racial exploitation, that underpinned the wealth of many nineteenth-century (particularly civic university) benefactors and is highlighted by their modern detractors. As far as 'good coming out of bad' is concerned, it is worth commenting on current staunch criticism of at least one major institution – the University of Oxford – for still being unrepresentative among its teaching staff of those races that suffered in the past from colonial practices, and also for its history courses being taught from a colonial perspective.[6]

The duty of an institution to uphold its reputation while acknowledging duties towards its benefactors: is there a conflict of interest?

John Shakeshaft, 'The expectations of benefactors and a responsibility to endow'

Victoria Harrison, 'The funder's perspective'

Universities well understand the imperative to raise funds from private philanthropic sources that are an important element in providing flexibility and a modicum of autonomy. Dependency on any single source of income can be dangerous, for every major funder has its imperative. Central government can require unacceptable political compliance. Major benefactors may try to impose controversial conditions. Research income from the corporate sector could move a university towards becoming a business. Reliance on fee income without adequate scholarship funding can disadvantage poor families. (We are today only too aware of all these concerns.) As a result, any institution that is able to raise money through philanthropy in a cost-effective manner is almost duty-bound – if it is concerned for the common good – to do so. For it is a significant element in income diversity. Moreover, there will be many projects that can only be realized through philanthropic funding.

It is the university's lead fundraiser who bears the brunt of managing the relationship between it and its benefactors. He or she must be janus-faced.

---

[6] This has been one of the major criticisms of the 'Rhodes Must Fall' and 'Common Ground' movements in Oxford.

On the one hand s/he must face outward to explain the university and its needs to those in the external world whose interest and involvement could be advantageous for the institution. On the other hand, the fundraiser must face inwards, diplomatically explaining and introducing appropriate prospective donors to individuals within the university where the potential personal chemistry seems most suitable for benefactor involvement. As the institution's employee, it is his or her role to secure as much private funding as possible for agreed projects without in any way embarrassing the university. This latter caveat is a golden rule.

Stories of where this has gone wrong are legion. Back in the relatively early days of the involvement of professionals in British university fundraising, as a newly arrived director of development at Oxford, I found a highly anxious senior management of the University faced with public criticism for having accepted a major donation for a named academic post from the grandson of an individual who had been a prominent Nazi and made his fortune through the exploitation of Jewish slave labour. A Jewish alumnus of the university had exposed the issue to the press, thereby causing the donor – who had thought he was helping to right a past family wrong through his benefaction – to rescind his financial commitment, causing not only embarrassment but also a considerable funding problem for the university.[7] Lessons were learned from this painful incident – principally the need for more stringent mechanisms for scrutinizing the nature of donor prospects and their potential gifts. The development office was required to investigate the nature of a prospect's source of wealth ahead of the acceptance of a major donation, with recourse to a distinguished academic standing committee where there were any doubts. This is now standard practice in respected universities as John Shakeshaft's essay makes clear, as is also the transparency of institutional investment policy.

Yet it cannot be a foolproof system. First, it can be tricky for development officers if elements of their institution pressurize them to ignore ethical issues in the interests of accepting funding for a favourite project. (Sometimes – against professional best practice – these officials are financially rewarded on the basis of funding they secure.) Second – as soon became clear to that Oxford team of fundraisers – there are few, if any, fortunes that have been made in ways that are wholly ethical by contemporary standards and cannot be challenged by some identity group or other. Third, any authority making judgements about sources of wealth can only do so on the basis of contemporary ethical imperatives. They cannot speak for the next generation that may take a different view about the morality of past

---

[7] See also Cannadine above, p. 3.

benefactors. Furthermore, senior fundraisers have a loyalty and, to some extent, duty to the institution's benefactors. Their duty to protect their institution should not mask this responsibility if they wish to encourage further major donations and to keep in good faith with former stakeholders such as alumni. Above all, the institutional leadership needs to agree, and commit publicly to the kind of community and society the university aims to be. Its public value system should be a touchstone for its relationship with its benefactors.

University museums and their benefactions

Laura N. K. Van Broekhoven, 'Calibrating relevance at the Pitt Rivers Museum'

Tiffany Jenkins, 'From objects of enlightenment to objects of apology: why you can't make amends for the past by plundering the present'

Benefactions to universities are not only monetary. They can be collections of books for libraries. They can be artefacts, housed in museums. University museums, whose directors and curators are university officers, are particularly connected with aspects of academic study and scholarship. They may have laboratories for research and analysis; they may display artefacts in order to teach; they may publish their research and findings. The Ashmolean Museum's cast gallery, for example, displays plaster casts of classical statues as working models of the 'real thing', located in Greece. Such museums usually welcome public access and involvement in their displays and work. Indeed, they require public engagement for community support, publicity and funding.

In recent years some donated collections to both university and national museums have presented ethical challenges linked to the politics of identity and anti-colonialism. These have also developed from late twentieth-century protests by, or on behalf of, historically underprivileged – often oppressed – elements in human society. Minority social groups, including African tribes and Native Americans, together with those that have taken up their cause, have objected to the way in which museums have displayed artefacts given by, and believed to be of interest to, archaeologists, anthropologists and collectors. Criticism includes a sense of patronization in the labelling. Another is a perceived lack of respect for human remains where these have been publicly displayed. Underlying the alleged distress has been a sense that dominant races, especially in a colonial era, have given no thought in these cases to very different cultural beliefs and patterns of minority human groups. The United States government's 1990 Native American Grave

Protection and Repatriation Act, in addressing this problem, has had the effect of encouraging today's Native Americans to enforce their indigenous rights by demanding the return of human remains relating to their ancestors. Museums such as the Denver Museum of Nature and Science subsequently returned nearly all such artefacts. The argument against this practice revolves around the removal of valuable evidence for scientists researching evolution, population movements and historic social structures and lifestyles.[8]

Concerns about disrespect arising from the exhibition of human remains have been an issue in the U.K. – for example, in connection with Oxford's Pitt Rivers Museum's shrunken heads or 'tsantas' from Latin America collected between 1871 and 1936, donated by various collectors, some of whom regarded them as 'exotic curiosities', others of whom found them a useful tool for archaeological or anthropological study.[9] As a result of such concerns, the museum community has worked hard, over the past decades, to ensure that educational and cultural information is communicated sensitively and that the displays are respectful both to visitors and to the dead.[10] As Laura Van Broekhoven illustrates, the Pitt Rivers Museum constantly undergoes 'critical introspection' about such sensitivities.[11]

In Britain the perception of patronization and disrespect tends to have been associated with the nation's colonial past and racial exploitation exhibited by colonial officials. As such there have also been strong and ongoing accusations of theft where artefacts were brought back to Britain at the whim of colonial rulers – notoriously, for example, in the case of the Benin bronzes from modern-day Nigeria, now displayed in the British Museum. Such museum displays have become a focus of past injustices in the same way that many commemorative statues have become symbols in identity politics.

[8] See, for example, T. Jenkins, 'Making amends to Native Americans may be endangering their history', *Spectator*, 15 Apr. 2017.

[9] 'Human remains in the Pitt Rivers Museum' <http://www.prm.ox.ac.uk> [accessed 16 Apr. 2018]. Public museums have usually formulated procedures for returning human remains of this kind when requested; for example, the Hunterian Museum, Glasgow has returned some Maori heads to a tribe in New Zealand.

[10] See also M. O'Hanlon, *The Pitt Rivers Museum: a World Within* (London and Oxford, 2014), pp. 91ff.

[11] See below, p. 73.

Broader issues: viewing and judging the past from the perspective of the present

Nicholas Draper, 'British universities and Caribbean slavery'

Anna Eavis and Howard Spencer, 'Risk and reputation: the London blue plaques scheme'

Brian Young, '"A dreary record of wickedness": moral judgement in history'

Physical memorials – statues of individuals, named buildings – are an important aspect of western culture that goes beyond historical symbolism. In a civic context, streets, squares and buildings are named after battles, dates and heroes in towns and cities all over Europe, from a *rue Napoléon* in even the smallest French village to ubiquitous statues of Garibaldi and Cavour throughout Italy. In English towns suburban development at the turn of the twentieth century often recalls a period of colonial history with a Mafeking Street or a Kimberley Avenue. These tangible images and constructions have become significant aspects of urban art and architecture, part of the street-scene, even sometimes regarded affectionately and comfortingly by regular passers-by who may not consider their historical significance.

But we are coming up against the unavoidable fact that practices that may generally have been judged morally acceptable in one society, at one particular moment in history, may well be considered differently at another. Twenty years ago it might have been said: 'but no-one would want to see a monument commemorating Hitler'. Now a different aspect of man's inhumanity to man, associated with inhumane and racist aspects of the long period of colonialism, has led to equal offence being given by monuments of erstwhile heroes of that era. And what complicates the discussion are issues of ethical relativism one of which is assessing the extent to which those who have benefitted from slavery are tainted.

At one end of the scale come the slave traders and slave owners whose whole way of life – business, living arrangements, position in colonial society – was based on ownership of slaves. A now notorious example of one who was a notable university benefactor is Christopher Codrington, whose wealth enabled his old college, All Souls, Oxford to found its magnificent library. At the other end of the scale come individuals who have – even unwittingly – benefitted indirectly as descendants of those who were compensated in the years following the Slavery Abolition Act, 1833. In between come traders in commodities produced as the result of slave labour, such as coffee, tea, sugar and cotton, on plantations owned by others; and transatlantic shippers whose cargo included such commodities probably among many others. Some of the founders of what became the universities of Manchester, Liverpool and Bristol come into this category. It is hard to believe that individuals in all these categories are equally guilty of complicity in slavery.

This in itself is a historical judgement. It touches on the issue of the extent to which historians should make moral judgements about those whom they study and write. It is the historian's role to explain the context in which past individuals lived and acted. But to what extent should they make moral judgements about their subjects rather than hiding behind the view of them as 'men of their times'? Contemporary historians have varying views about this. Eamon Duffy, Cambridge Professor of the History of Christianity, writing about the killing of protestant martyrs in a pre-Enlightenment age, has argued that

> The historian's task is to explore that other country, the past, and to bring back news of how its people differed from, as well as resembled ourselves … indignation at the motives and actions of the long dead is a poor aid to understanding. I have tried to set it aside in dealing with the dauntingly different values of those times.[12]

On the other hand, Denis Mack Smith, historian of a more recent era, nineteenth- and twentieth-century Italy, felt that 'he is a coward or a dullard who does not risk some interim judgements on the course of history'.[13]

There is no temporal gold standard – certainly not our current era – in terms of ethical judgements about benefactors who endow universities. Our own descendants will have their own, very likely differing, views about the ways in which the benefactors of our age have acquired their fortunes. In the circumstances of fifty or one hundred years time, they may well feel dubious about the basis of current wealth. Hopefully, they will continue to feel that private investment in universities is important as a public good.

[12] Interview with Michael Berkeley, B.B.C. 3 programme, *Private Passions*, 14 Dec. 2014. Here he was particularly referring to the large-scale burning of Protestants in the 16th century by Mary Tudor.
[13] Quoted in his obituary by J. Foot, *The Guardian*, 8 Aug. 2017, referring to Mack Smith's book, *Cavour and Garibaldi 1860: a Study in Political Conflict* (Cambridge, 1954).

3. The English civic universities: endowments and the commemoration of benefactors

H. S. Jones

Universities are by no means the only institutions caught up in current arguments about the commemoration and the de-commemoration of benefactors and former worthies, but they are central to these controversies.[1] That is partly for an obvious reason: universities educate students, and student political culture has long been an arena in which identity politics and culture wars have been vigorously fought. It is hardly surprising that student activists wanting to secure reparation for past injustice – most obviously, the injustice of slavery – should have turned their attention towards their own universities. Still, I think that is only a partial answer. The university as an institution is old, and so too are many of the world's most celebrated universities. Clark Kerr of the University of California once calculated that about seventy of the eighty-five oldest institutions of the western world are universities, and more recent studies have shown the benefits relative antiquity continues to confer on universities.[2] So there are questions to be asked about why universities – more than other kinds of institutions – derive benefit from age, and why they have often chosen funding models that tend to privilege antiquity. This short paper begins with a historical consideration of these issues, before moving on to examine how universities in the past and present have deployed their heritage and continue to do so.

Endowments and the Victorians

The critique of endowments was a fundamental issue in Victorian politics, public policy and political thought.[3] It was really central to what divided

---

[1] D. G. Faust, 'Recognizing slavery at Harvard', in *The Harvard Crimson* <http://www.thecrimson.com/article/2016/3/30/faust-harvard-slavery/> [accessed 25 Feb. 2018].

[2] A. Geuna, 'The internationalisation of European universities: a return to medieval roots', *Minerva*, xxxvi (1998), 253–70.

[3] A key work here is L. Goldman, 'The defection of the middle class: the Endowed Schools Act, the Liberal party, and the 1874 general election', in *Politics and Culture in Victorian*

H. S. Jones, 'The English civic universities: endowments and the commemoration of benefactors', in *Dethroning historical reputations: universities, museums and the commemoration of benefactors*, ed. J. Pellew and L. Goldman (2018), pp. 25–34.

whigs and tories in the 1830s, and Liberals and Conservatives in the era of Gladstone and Disraeli and beyond. Municipal corporations, Irish bishoprics, the cathedral chapters, parochial charities, the major public schools, the endowed grammar schools, the City livery companies, and – of course – the universities of Oxford and Cambridge were all the subject of reformers' attentions and in most cases were the subject of royal commissions and legislative action.[4] Conservatives defended what Disraeli in 1873 termed 'the sacredness of Endowments', whereas Liberals lambasted endowments either as obstacles to a competitive market or as appropriations of what was properly considered public property for private or in any case arbitrary purposes.[5]

Still, the universities emerged unscathed from this assault, and in some ways they benefited from the reform of endowed institutions. Yes, the endowments of Oxford and Cambridge colleges were remodelled, in particular to open up their benefits to non-Anglicans, but also to free colleges from obligations to particular localities and thus to allow them to become more meritocratic.[6] But there was no attempt to disendow these collegiate foundations which were in some cases very wealthy; nor was there any attempt to divert their endowments to newer universities and colleges. And universities gained in many other ways. Just as in the late middle ages and the Reformation the Oxford and Cambridge colleges often benefited from the appropriation of the property of suppressed religious houses, so in the nineteenth century universities were net gainers from the assault on historic endowments. This occurred in at least five distinct ways.

First, the revenues from suppressed Irish bishoprics were diverted in the 1830s to support education, especially higher education, in Ireland. This was a famously controversial measure which both split the whig cabinet and was the proximate cause of the formation of the Oxford Movement, since the defence of the property of the Irish church was the subject of John Keble's

---

Britain: Essays in Memory of Colin Matthew, ed. P. Ghosh and L. Goldman (Oxford, 2006), pp. 118–35.

[4] The classic source is D. Owen, *English Philanthropy 1660–1960* (Cambridge, Mass., 1965), pt. 3.

[5] Hansard, *Parliamentary Debates*, cciv (20 March 1873), col. 1944. Conversely, Gladstone aroused fierce controversy with his 1863 budget speech, in which he announced a proposal to tax charities' endowment income, a proposal he was obliged to withdraw (M. Daunton, *Trusting Leviathan: the Politics of Taxation in Britain, 1799–1914* (Cambridge, 2007), pp. 211–13, 232–3).

[6] There is an accessible account in L. W. B. Brockliss, *The University of Oxford: a History* (Oxford, 2016), ch. 9, to supplement the authoritative study *The History of the University of Oxford*, vii: *Nineteenth-Century Oxford, Part 1*, ed. M. G. Brock and M. C. Curthoys (Oxford, 1997), especially ch. 23.

famous Assize Sermon of 1833. This denounced the whig government's Irish Church Temporalities Bill, which proposed to suppress ten bishoprics, as a breach of faith with donors and an act of 'national apostasy'.[7]

Second, the extremely wealthy chapter of Durham cathedral supported the establishment of the University of Durham, primarily to ensure that the endowments, by being deployed to meet a clear public need, were retained for church purposes. The new university worked hard to ensure that its degrees were confined to Anglicans, but the whig government insisted that it should open its classes if not its degrees to dissenters, and secured a provision whereby non-conformist Durham students could qualify for London University degrees. The university thus became something more than a mere Anglican enclave, and indeed a recent study has shown that the familiar picture of Durham in its early decades as a reactionary failure does not do justice to the educational innovations it introduced.[8]

Third, some Oxford and Cambridge colleges, anticipating the late Victorian and Edwardian university extension movement, supported the development of new civic colleges. This practice was first advocated by the influential educational reformer, and later bishop, John Percival. His pamphlet, *The Connection of the Universities and the Great Towns* (1873), written when he was headmaster of Clifton College, Bristol, urged the suppression of college fellowships to provide for provincial chairs, and it was in Bristol that this policy came closest to fruition.[9] University College, Bristol, founded in 1876, was funded in part from the endowments of two Oxford colleges, Balliol and New College, which each gave annual grants of £300 for five years to get the new college off the ground, in the absence of substantial local benefactors.[10]

Fourth, the new civic colleges, and Oxford and Cambridge too, received grants from the City livery companies. The companies stepped up their charitable donations in response to growing public criticism from London radicals of their misuse of their endowments to support gluttonous dinners. Sometimes these grants were specifically tied to the development of departments of applied science: thus sustained funding from the Clothworkers' Company enabled Yorkshire College, Leeds, to

---

[7] B. Hilton, *A Mad, Bad, and Dangerous People? England 1783–1846* (Oxford, 2006), pp. 468, 496; also R. Brent, *Liberal Anglican Politics: Whiggery, Religion, and Reform 1830–1841* (Oxford, 1987), ch. 2.

[8] M. P. Andrews, 'Durham University: the last of the ancient universities and the first of the new' (unpublished University of Oxford D.Phil. thesis, 2016).

[9] Owen, *English Philanthropy*, p. 366; J. Sadler, 'Percival, John (1834–1918)', in *O.D.N.B.* <https://doi.org/10.1093/ref:odnb/35471> [accessed 2 Oct. 2017].

[10] K. Vernon, *Universities and the State in England, 1850–1939* (Abingdon, 2004), p. 104.

establish a department of tinctorial chemistry and dyeing and a department of textile industry. In total the University of Leeds had received well over half a million pounds from the Clothworkers by the 1950s.[11] At Oxford, the Drapers' Company financed the Electrical Laboratory (now the Clarendon Laboratory), a new building for the Radcliffe Science Library, and the establishment of the department of social anthropology. Several livery companies also established exhibitions for poor non-collegiate students.[12] The companies – the Drapers and the Goldsmiths in particular – were also handsome donors (£33,000 out of a total of £150,000 raised) to the Oxford Re-endowment Fund. That fund, launched in 1907 by Lord Curzon as chancellor of the University, was itself testament to the resilience of the endowment principle at the start of the twentieth century.[13]

Fifth and finally, the City Parochial Charities Act of 1883 authorized commissioners to divert the endowments of many parochial charities to the support of the technical colleges of London, some of which later became polytechnics and in turn universities. The commissioners normally established schemes that required matching funding, and this helped leverage not only public subscription, but also substantial and ongoing commitments from livery companies, notably the Haberdashers and the Drapers.[14] Institutions that were given financial stability by schemes of this kind included the Regent Street Polytechnic, ancestor of the University of Westminster, Goldsmiths' Institute (later College, and now Goldsmiths University of London), and the People's Palace, forerunner of Queen Mary University of London, which was generously supported by the Drapers' Company.[15] So the economy of higher education, even in the new institutions, was powerfully shaped by the legacy of ancient endowments.

The civic universities

Not only did universities and colleges old and new benefit from the redeployment of endowments both ecclesiastical and secular, but – crucially for the purposes of this volume – new endowments leveraged from private benefactors were critical to the political economy of the new civic colleges which in the early years of the twentieth century were transformed into

[11] Owen, *English Philanthropy*, p. 367.
[12] *The History of the University of Oxford*, vii: *Nineteenth-Century Oxford, Part 2*, ed. M. G. Brock and M. C. Curthoys (Oxford, 2000), pp. 461, 486, 503, 640, 196.
[13] Owen, *English Philanthropy*, p. 355. But the fund itself fell short of its target of £250,000.
[14] D. Owen, 'The City parochial charities: the "Dead Hand" in late Victorian London', *Jour. British Studies*, i (1962), 115–35.
[15] S. Webb, *London Education* (1904), ch. 4.

civic universities. Think, in particular, of Manchester and Liverpool, of Leeds and Sheffield, of Birmingham and Bristol. It is a striking fact that the vigorous assault mounted on the misuse of historical endowments by Liberal and Radical reformers in Victorian England did not turn the business communities of such cities as Manchester and Liverpool against the idea of furnishing universities with permanent endowments. By 1890 Owens College, Manchester, derived 45 per cent of its income from endowments – more than it derived from student fees.[16] The proportion diminished thereafter, as the colleges expanded into universities, their costs grew, and public support was at last forthcoming. But new endowments could still be extracted, certainly at the time of the conversion to university status in 1903–4. Civic pride was a crucial motive: indeed, university status was deemed necessary in part in order to increase the flow of new endowments. The very term 'civic universities', coined at this very time, is resonant of a rich intellectual and cultural context in which citizenship grounded in the city became a centrally important concept in British social thought. Civic universities were not just universities *in* the city, but universities *of* the city.[17]

It is worth identifying some of the largest benefactors. John Owens founded the college that was to bear his name at Manchester with a legacy of almost £100,000. One subsequent benefactor matched this: in 1876 the German-born engineer Charles Beyer left £100,000 in his will, establishing science chairs and funding a new science building, and overall between 1850 and 1914 the College and subsequently the University received in total almost £700,000 in substantial gifts (£10,000 or more).[18] Particularly notable donors included the engineer and machine tool manufacturer, Sir Joseph Whitworth, who personally and through his residuary legatees gave Owens College a sum totalling around £150–160,000.[19] One of the residuary legatees, Richard Copley Christie, not only used his share of the Whitworth estate to fund the construction of the Whitworth Hall for public ceremonies (£56,839), but also from his own resources built the first College library (£23,000). John Rylands and his widow Enriqueta gave a total of almost £96,000 between 1889 and 1909, quite apart from the vast sum – around £1 million – that Enriqueta spent on building, endowing and acquiring collections for the John Rylands Library, founded in 1900 in memory of her

---

[16] W. Whyte, *Redbrick: a Social and Architectural History of Britain's Civic Universities* (Oxford, 2015), p. 139.

[17] A powerful and influential statement of this position can be found in R. Muir, *Plea for a Liverpool University* (Liverpool, 1901).

[18] Owen, *English Philanthropy*, p. 364.

[19] E. Fiddes, *Chapters in the History of Owens College and of Manchester University 1851– 1914* (Manchester, 1937), p. 126 n. 1.

husband, the wealthiest manufacturer in Victorian Manchester. This was an endowed part of the library separate from the university, which did not acquire it until the 1970s, but it was a major component of the academic infrastructure of the city.[20]

Manchester was the best endowed of the civic universities, but a similar pattern can be found elsewhere. In Birmingham, Sir Josiah Mason gave some £200,000 in 1875 to establish Mason Science College. In Bristol, H. O. Wills gave £100,000 to enable University College, Bristol, to establish itself as the University of Bristol; and his two sons gave the University a further £500,000 between 1913 and 1920. Liverpool had no donors of that magnitude, but was highly successful in mobilizing the business community to raise a large number of smaller donations: a gift of £10,000 was sufficient to endow a chair, as in the case of the chair of economic science founded by the radical Liberal M.P. Sir John Brunner, of the great chemical firm Brunner Mond.

Can these universities, or their successors, be proud of their benefactors? Is there anything in the suggestion that the universities of Manchester, Liverpool and Bristol are built on the profits of slavery? It is certainly true that some and quite possibly many of the big donors to these incipient universities made their fortunes from trade in tobacco, sugar and cotton – the three main products of the slave plantations of the American South and Cuba. In the case of Manchester – Cottonopolis – we know that manufacturing was highly dependent on the produce of the plantations of the American South: hence the famous Lancashire cotton famine, caused by the blockade of Southern ports by the federal navy during the American Civil War. Owens and Rylands, among other major donors (but not Beyer and Whitworth), made their fortunes largely or wholly through cotton manufacture and overseas trade in cotton goods. How we should interpret this fact is open to debate, since the cotton industry in particular and trades associated with it were, of course, hugely important to the nineteenth-century British economy, and modern Britain is shaped in so many ways by the wealth generated by Victorian trade and industry.

The ethics of buying slave-produced goods, for consumption or for trade or manufacture, are also complex. Whether a cotton manufacturer, for instance, could be said to have profited from slavery, depends in part upon assumptions about the economic consequences of slave labour. Was slavery an economically rational system driven by the dictates of capitalism? Or,

---

[20] Notable benefactions to Owens College and the Victoria University of Manchester are listed in H. B. Charlton, *Portrait of a University 1851–1951: to Commemorate the Centenary of Manchester University* (Manchester, 1951), Appendix III, pp. 143–7.

to the contrary, was slave labour in fact inefficient, as many proponents of abolition and many economic historians have argued?[21] This empirical question is clearly relevant to the kind of moral judgement we make. If slave labour was inefficient, then those who traded in slave-produced cotton, sugar or tobacco were certainly implicated in the political economy of slavery, but it is not clear that they profited from it, since their raw materials might have been cheaper in the absence of slavery. Clearly there are degrees of culpability, and there were groups in early Victorian Britain – in particular, the Quaker free-produce movement – who argued that trading in or even consuming the produce of slave labour was morally equivalent to trading in slaves or owning slaves.[22] But the contrary view was held by many morally serious people, including abolitionists, and in the case of cotton in particular, there was hardly any free produce to compete with slave produce.[23]

This is a question which will no doubt continue to generate debate as the ethical consumption movement gains pace. It is significant that attention has so far focused more on those such as the Wills family who made their fortunes from tobacco – perhaps because it is now seen as ethically dubious because of modern medical knowledge – and those, such as the Tate family, who traded in sugar, another product of central importance to the ethical consumption movement. There has been less attention to those who made their fortunes from cotton, a product which is less significant to that movement. That points to the complexity of the issues at stake, and to the deployment of considerations that could not have been available to the

---

[21] This is a long-standing controversy among economists and economic historians, stretching back to the work of the Victorian economist John Elliott Cairnes, who argued that slavery inhibited economic growth in the American South. Consensus is elusive.

[22] See, for example, L. Billington, 'British humanitarians and American cotton, 1840–1860', *Jour. Amer. Studies*, xi (1977), 313–34; R. Huzzey, 'The moral geography of British anti-slavery responsibilities', *Trans. Royal Hist. Soc.*, xxii (2012), 111–39. The latter draws out effectively why most anti-slavery campaigners did not feel moral revulsion at traded goods originating with slave labour.

[23] Interestingly, campaigners for the renaming of the Wills Tower at Bristol University have conflated the difference between trading in slaves and trading in the produce of slave labour: e.g., 'Bristol university Wills Memorial Building keeps "slave trade" name', *B.B.C. News*, 4 July 2017 <http://www.bbc.co.uk/news/uk-england-bristol-40497882> [accessed 30 Sept. 2017]. Likewise, 'Students inspired by Rhodes Must Fall campaign demand Bristol University change name of Wills Tower over "slave trade" links', *Daily Telegraph*, 28 March 2017 <http://www.telegraph.co.uk/education/2017/03/28/students-inspired-rhodes-must-fall-campaign-demand-bristol-university/> [accessed 28 March 2017] and 'Ghosts of Bristol's shameful slave past haunt its graceful landmarks', *The Observer*, 2 Apr. 2017 <https://www.theguardian.com/uk-news/2017/apr/02/bristol-slave-trade-ties-wills-building-colston-hall-rename-petition> [accessed 2 Apr. 2017]. The Wills family were certainly not slave traders.

historical agents, as well as considerations that were available to them. On the whole I remain to be convinced that the Wills family, Sir Henry Tate, John Owens, Edward Langworthy and the rest were the moral equivalents of Cecil Rhodes.

Universities and heritage

For me, there is an important issue here about why universities – certainly private universities in the U.S.A., but U.K. universities too – use endowments in particular (rather than benefactions more generally) as a key feature of their business model.[24] Of course, a substantial proportion of university endowments today – unlike in the nineteenth century – are not endowments in the strict sense: they are quasi-endowments, since the capital is expendable if the universities so choose.[25] But they seek as a matter of policy to build up their permanent capital to a level where it produces a substantial income from interest. That is obviously a very different kind of choice from that which would be involved if they chose to spend major gifts over a fixed period (say five to ten years). This choice clearly has a lot to do with an aspiration to institutional permanence, indeed immortality, and that in turn stems from a distinctive (though not unique) characteristic of universities: that they derive great reputational benefit from being old. Long-term commemoration of benefactors is bound up with the quest for durability. Universities perceive a need for endowments to underpin their permanence, while that permanence reinforces their appeal to prospective benefactors. The benefits of permanence and antiquity remain strong. We live in an age of 'neo-liberal' management which privileges the new and innovative, but at the same time universities' marketing departments have become increasingly conscious of the benefits that they can derive from their heritage, and often this involves tenuous claims to age. Liverpool John Moores University, for instance, was established in 1823, Leeds Beckett in 1824, the University of Central Lancashire in 1828, and Cardiff Metropolitan University in 1865.[26]

My own institution, The University of Manchester, provides a fascinating case in point. It was the product of a merger in 2004 of the old University of Manchester (formally named the Victoria University of Manchester) and U.M.I.S.T., the University of Manchester Institute of Science and

---

[24] This question is raised by H. Hansmann, 'Why do universities have endowments?', *Jour. Legal Studies*, xix (1990), 3–42.

[25] This point is made by Hansmann, pp. 8–9.

[26] All from the United Kingdom Education Advisory Service website <http://www.ukeas.com> [accessed 8 Oct. 2017].

Technology. The resulting university was self-consciously new, driven by a vision of a radical culture shift, and hence a step-change in performance, achieved in part through the erasure of old institutional structures. Its novelty was signalled by the aggressively capitalized definite article in the name, and by the appointment of a pugnacious Australian president and vice-chancellor, who dropped the national anthem from degree ceremonies, since it was regarded as out of line with the ethos of a global university. This was the academic equivalent of France in 1790, except that whereas the French revolutionaries swept provinces from the map in favour of departments, the academic revolutionaries swept departments away, to be replaced by huge interdisciplinary schools. This self-conscious modernity sat oddly with the new logo, which signalled the university's origins in 1824 – a date whose significance had escaped the notice of historians of universities, but which was, in fact, the date of the formation of the Manchester Mechanics' Institute, a forerunner of U.M.I.S.T. And a few years later the University, discovering the reputational benefits of heritage, created the post of University historian and heritage manager – the first post of its kind in a British university, and held by Dr. James Hopkins.[27]

The Manchester case is an extreme one, but it exemplifies an important point. In spite of the apparent triumph of neo-liberal managerialism, universities are institutional palimpsests, whose curricular structures, built environments, and traditions bear the imprint of the academic politics of the past. That is not an argument for preserving the entire legacy of the past, but it does constitute an argument for a presumption in favour of the preservation of that legacy. Universities, I suggest, are stronger and more interesting for having distinctive individual identities shaped by their pasts. The survival of names commemorating benefactors and worthies of the past also signals something of the moral complexity of institutional histories.

I conclude with a comment about commemoration and naming practices.[28] There are many ways in which benefactors may be commemorated, but naming *universities* after them did not become part of the British practice until the ending of the binary divide in 1992: Heriot-Watt in 1966 is the only example – actually half an example – before John Moores University and Robert Gordon University in 1992. Colleges were different – although naming colleges after founders did not become common in Oxford and Cambridge until the twentieth century. The civic colleges of the Victorian

---

[27] <http://www.manchester.ac.uk/discover/history-heritage/contact-about/> [accessed 8 Oct. 2017].

[28] Since this paper was drafted in March 2017 for the conference at the Institute of Historical Research, I have had the opportunity to listen to an illuminating presentation on university naming practices by Keith Vernon of the University of Central Lancashire.

period were quite often named after benefactors – Owens College, Mason College, Firth College – but, interestingly, when they acquired university status they eschewed that kind of identification with a founder. One reason for this was that the new universities aspired to be coterminous with higher education and learning in the cities in which they were located: not a university in Manchester or Birmingham or Sheffield, but *the* University of Manchester, of Birmingham, of Sheffield. Prior to 1992, the only city with more than one university was London, where City University and (out at Uxbridge) Brunel coexisted with the University of London.

There is a stark contrast between British naming practices prior to 1992 and American practice. Named universities are common in the U.S.A., where founders such as John Harvard, Elihu Yale, Ezra Cornell, Johns Hopkins, Leland Stanford, James Buchanan Duke, John Purdue, Cornelius Vanderbilt, and many others are commemorated in the names of the universities they founded. It should be added, however, that another common practice in the U.S.A. is for universities to be named after a famous person rather than a benefactor: examples include Brown, Rutgers, George Washington, George Mason and Emory. Even this practice was unknown in England before the former Leicester Polytechnic chose to name itself after Simon de Montfort. De Montfort was not an uncontroversial choice of name, however, since the great proto-parliamentarian was also deeply implicated in the persecution of the Jews. That raises a further point by way of conclusion. The reputations of 'great men' (and women) are open to historical revision and re-evaluation, just as much as those of wealthy benefactors are, but there is this difference. When we name a building, a chair, or a university after a great man or woman, we assert their worthiness, whereas when we name one after a wealthy benefactor we acknowledge the gift, and recognize a wise decision, but (I suggest) do not necessarily assert the personal worthiness of the benefactor.

4. Donors to an imperial project: Randlords as benefactors to the Royal School of Mines, Imperial College of Science and Technology

Jill Pellew

There is much discomfort today about and within institutions that benefited from profits made by exploiting human beings in the age of imperial aggression. Fortunes made in the glory days of British trade and colonial enterprise have been particularly attacked – famously by the 'Rhodes Must Fall' movement which has focused on the racist attitudes and overweening sense of British superiority displayed in South Africa after diamonds and gold were discovered there in the late nineteenth century. This movement's name refers to its objective of pulling down statues erected in an earlier age to celebrate an individual now vilified. There may, therefore, be interest in the story of the major benefactions that derived from South African wealth at the turn of the twentieth century: those of Alfred Beit and Julius Wernher to the Royal School of Mines (R.S.M.), an important component of Imperial College of Science and Technology, founded in 1907.[1]

The establishment of Imperial College on a grand site in South Kensington was partly the brainchild of the politician and educationalist R. B. (Viscount) Haldane who, despite his work as secretary of state for war and later lord chancellor in the Liberal governments of 1905 and 1908, was continuously interested and involved in the reform and progress of universities. Above all, he worked with social reformers, in particular Sidney Webb, to reform the University of London, which until the very end of the nineteenth century was effectively an examining board for other institutions, rather than an academic entity. 'Higher education, Haldane believed, played a vital role in national efficiency because it was both the agent of progress – moral, scientific, and economic – and was the means of social development'.[2] One

---

[1] The name was changed to 'Imperial College of Science, Technology and Medicine' in 1988 after a merger with St. Mary's Hospital Medical School (and subsequently other London medical schools). Since the granting of its institutional autonomy in 2007, it has been known as 'Imperial College, London'.

[2] H. C. G. Matthew, 'Haldane, Richard Burdon, Viscount Haldane (1856–1928)', in

J. Pellew, 'Donors to an imperial project: Randlords as benefactors to the Royal School of Mines, Imperial College of Science and Technology', in *Dethroning historical reputations: universities, museums and the commemoration of benefactors*, ed. J. Pellew and L. Goldman (2018), pp. 35–46.

of his major roles in the development of the University of London was in the creation of a new British technical university 'fit for the metropolis of Empire'. For this, his model, which he visited in 1901, was the great Prussian *Technische Hochschule* at Charlottenburg, founded in 1879.[3]

The origins of the project harked back to the 1851 Great Exhibition whose commissioners were encouraged to direct its considerable profits towards the prince consort's dream of increasing the means of industrial education by extending the influence of science and art. This was subsequently given impetus by public concern about Britain's lagging behind her Continental competitors in industrial output following the 1867 Paris International Exposition. In due course, development crystallized on the area in South Kensington, south of Hyde Park. From 1884 the City and Guilds Institute, founded by a group of City livery companies to provide a system of technical education, was housed in a grand Waterhouse building along the west side of Exhibition Road. Meanwhile, from 1881 the R.S.M. and the Royal College of Science (R.C.S.) – each of which had had its own separate historical development in central London – were housed together in the Huxley building, further down and on the other side of Exhibition Road. By the end of the century this accommodation had become inadequate and they were unable to realise their scientific and technical potential.[4] The challenge involved bringing these three separate institutions together to form an Imperial Charlottenburg in South Kensington, hopefully as part of the University of London. It was a hugely ambitious project, which involved changing the constitutional status of the R.C.S. and R.S.M., the acquisition of additional real estate, and – above all – securing funding, both public and private. None of these things could be done without high-level support.

Haldane was a champion at making a cross-party case to leading politicians, including Lord Rosebery, patron of the Liberal imperialists, and Arthur Balfour, Conservative prime minister from 1902–5. He claimed even to have convinced Edward VII.[5] As for real estate, the commissioners were well disposed to grant the project the last available parcel of land left from

---

O.D.N.B. <https://doi.org/10.1093/ref:odnb/33643> [accessed 14 July 2017]. Later Haldane was to chair the Royal Commission on London University between 1909 and 1913.

[3] E. Ashby and M. Anderson, *Portrait of Haldane at Work on Education* (1974), pp. 45, 49.

[4] For more extensive background to the creation of an Imperial College of Science and Technology in South Kensington, see J. Pellew, 'A Metropolitan University fit for Empire: the role of private benefaction in the early history of the London School of Economics and Political Science and Imperial College of Science and Technology, 1895–1930', *History of Universities*, xxvi (2012), 217–31. See also A. R. Hall, *Science for Industry: a Short History of the Imperial College of Science and Technology* (1982).

[5] Ashby and Anderson, *Portrait of Haldane at Work*, p. 51.

1851 at the northern end of Exhibition Road. This was to become the new site of an enlarged R.S.M. Now major capital was required for suitable buildings to rehouse and extensively equip an ambitiously modernized R.C.S. and R.S.M. Both capital endowment and recurrent funding were needed for additional staff and student scholarships. There were three principal sources of finance: the tax-payer at both local and national level (through the London County Council (L.C.C.) and by treasury grant); the corporate world of the City of London; and private individuals. Haldane began working on the treasury to pledge £20,000 towards the projected institution. But the project was fragile. At that date, the total annual treasury contribution towards new English university colleges en route to becoming autonomous institutions was in its infancy, amounting to some £27,000.[6] The founding of new civic universities had depended on the enterprise and finance of private individuals with modest support from local authorities; and the key to this whole enterprise was going to be the securing of major private financial commitment.

The timing was propitious. There was an obvious source of wealth that related particularly to the R.S.M. aspect of the project. The successful exploitation of diamond and gold mines in southern Africa in the last quarter of the nineteenth century had led to unprecedented fortunes among the so-called 'Randlords', some of whom had settled with their fortunes in London and become part of the Establishment. Mining engineering was, of course, the essential means by which these millionaires had made their fortunes and they well understood the urgent need for a stream of experts in mining techniques as mine managers. Imperial College had just the right tone, not least with its royal connections going back to Prince Albert's promotion of the 1851 Exhibition. Who could be a more obvious source of funding? In May 1901 Haldane called on the London partners of the firm Wernher, Beit & Co. in order to interest them in his project.

The key partners, Julius Wernher (1850–1912) and Alfred Beit (1853–1906), were of German origin. Wernher, son of a distinguished railway engineer from an old protestant family in Hesse, had a commercial education and worked in a Frankfurt bank before going to Paris to work for 'the greatest and wealthiest' diamond merchant, Théodore Porgès, who sent Wernher out into the field in 1872. Highly successful, he became a partner in Porgès's firm in Kimberley in the Orange Free State in 1873, and later head of a powerful mining consortium. Personally attributing his success to a steady approach

---

[6] Ashby and Anderson, *Portrait of Haldane at Work*, p. 76. For further details, see C. H. Shinn, *Paying the Piper: the Development of the University Grants Committee 1919–46* (Falmer, 1986), pp. 22ff.

to the rackety, crisis-ridden business of diamond mining, he became 'trusted and acknowledged as a leader, as much for his integrity of character as for his intellectual power'.[7] Alfred Beit, son of a Hamburg merchant from a Portuguese Sephardic Jewish family that had converted to Lutheranism, entered the diamond trade in Amsterdam as a young man before being sent out to South Africa in 1875. Beit possessed remarkable qualities that soon marked him out in the diamond business: a prodigious memory, sound judgement about the quality of diamonds, and 'the ability to solve financial questions swiftly and soundly … [knowing] how to reduce the most tangled and complicated matters to their essentials and to express them in the simplest formula'.[8] By the early 1880s he was associated with Wernher in Kimberley. The European base for these business activities was London where, during the 1880s, Wernher began to direct the operations of Jules Porgès & Co. He was involved in establishing the London Diamond Syndicate to stabilize the price of diamonds. On the retirement of Porgès, Beit joined Wernher and in early 1890 Wernher, Beit & Co. of London was incorporated. The relationship between Wernher and Beit was 'deep, based originally on their common nationality and appreciation of each other's business abilities'.[9]

Meanwhile, Beit's attention was drawn to gold-mining activity in the Transvaal where he established his own firm, in which his younger brother Otto also became involved, successfully pioneering new techniques of deep-shaft mining. He was the first to recognize the value of first-class mining engineers.[10] As part of his activity on the Rand he became a close friend and business partner of Cecil Rhodes to whom, in 1888, he lent a substantial amount of money for the formation of De Beers Consolidated Mines. It was a complementary partnership. Rhodes, 'the intellectual posturer', admired the mental agility of the shy, gauche Beit who 'envied and loved' Rhodes's 'commanding and leonine personality'.[11] Beit, Wernher and Rhodes were the leaders of a complex of men that controlled half the deep-level mining operations by 1895. These men depended on an African workforce; and by that time diamond and gold-mining had become an underground (rather than an open-cast) activity, involving a highly exploitative, closed compound system of controlling and cheaply paying African labourers. Health conditions in those mines were horrendous enough to have caused

[7] I. D. Colvin, 'Wernher, Sir Julius Charles, first baronet (1850–1912)', rev. Maryna Fraser, in *O.D.N.B.* <https://doi.org/10.1093/ref:odnb/36834> [accessed 20 July 2017].

[8] P. H. Emden, *Jews of Britain: a Series of Biographies* (1944), p. 409.

[9] Colvin, 'Wernher, Sir Julius Charles'.

[10] C. W. Boyd, 'Beit, Alfred (1853–1906)', rev. Ian Phimister, in *O.D.N.B.* <https://doi.org/10.1093/ref:odnb/30676> [accessed 20 July 2017].

[11] G. Wheatcroft, *The Randlords: the Men who Made South Africa* (1985), p. 50.

Wernher – much later, in 1909 – to bring in a leading British bacteriologist to advise on improvements which eventually led to a mass inoculation scheme between 1914 and 1918.[12]

Legendary wealth was accumulated through this activity. In the mid 1890s Beit was alleged to be the richest man in the world with shareholdings of some £10 million.[13] The power that such wealth bestowed became closely linked to aggressive imperial ambition. In 1890 Rhodes became prime minister of the Cape. Beit became a director of the British South Africa Company, whose aim was British colonial expansion in southern Africa, and he was notoriously involved in the unsuccessful Jameson Raid in 1895–6. His role in setting up Dr. Starr Jameson with an armed force, in order to stimulate insurrection and the overthrow of the [Boer] South African Republic in the Transvaal, was publicly exposed by a house of commons committee of inquiry by which he was censured. Rhodes was forced to resign as prime minister of the Cape. Beit – deeply antipathetic to publicity – suffered a nervous breakdown and was forced to resign his directorship of the British South Africa Company.[14]

Interestingly, this episode did not destroy his metropolitan social standing.[15] By the 1890s both Wernher and Beit had established themselves in London and eventually, in 1898, they both became British citizens. As members of the new plutocracy, known disparagingly as 'Randlords', they were subject to 'political malice and religious, racial and social prejudice'.[16] Part of this was due to their German and (in Beit's case) Jewish origins and links. The association with the Jameson Raid was dimly regarded. But, as David Cannadine points out, the major aspect of suspicion derived from the fact that these newcomers to an established society possessed wealth that enabled them to imitate the lifestyle and mores of the former leaders of society – the landed aristocracy, now severely weakened by the decline in the value of land and rents. They selected the smart West End of London for their homes – Wernher in Piccadilly and Beit in Park Lane – where they developed a passion for collecting pictures and other works of art. Wernher also purchased a country seat at Luton Hoo in Bedfordshire. Beit remained a bachelor and is described by his biographer as 'shy and retiring to excess

---

[12] Colvin, 'Wernher, Sir Julius Charles'.

[13] R. Trevelyan, *Grand Dukes and Diamonds: the Wernhers of Luton Hoo* (1981), p. 87.

[14] He allegedly drafted a will leaving £1 million to anyone who had suffered as a result of the Raid (Trevelyan, *Grand Dukes and Diamonds*, p. 93).

[15] Wernher distrusted Rhodes, was much less close to him than Beit and was not closely implicated in the Jameson Raid.

[16] D. Cannadine, *Decline and Fall of the British Aristocracy* (New Haven, Conn. and London, 1990), p. 345f.

... devoid of social ambition and ... little known beyond a small circle of intimates who included Rosebery and Haldane'.[17] Nevertheless, his lifestyle marked him out as one of the 'Randlords'. Key to becoming part of the smart set was proximity to the royal world of Edward VII, since their wealth enabled them to join a circle of donors to the king's favourite causes, often medical.[18] Their philanthropic activity earned them public honours: in the case of Wernher and Otto Beit, baronetcies.

The outcome of Haldane's visit to Wernher, Beit & Co. in 1901 proved to be a linchpin of the developing 'Charlottenburg' scheme. Afterwards, he reported to Webb that he had effectively diverted a prospective pledge of £100,000 being discussed for University College (clearly of less interest in his University of London plans) to his own project:

> I have undertaken to prepare a scheme for a Committee or body of Trustees to *begin* our big scheme. They will give us £100,000 to start it, and help us to get more ... I believe W.B. & Co. will give much more than £100,000 really.[19]

Haldane not only secured a major financial pledge but also the active involvement of the donors – particularly Wernher – in the scheme as it developed. Two significant events moved it forward. In June 1903 Rosebery wrote a letter to *The Times* proposing the creation of a 'metallurgical college', on the same day that a public fund, the Bessemer Memorial Fund, was launched in high style at the Mansion House in order to raise £20,000 for a laboratory to equip a new building for the R.S.M. This appeal became a grand and public affair (with a lead donation from Andrew Carnegie) to which many firms whose business related to the mining industry responded.[20] Meanwhile, Rosebery's public letter yielded the required response. Partly through pressure from Haldane's fervent ally, Sidney Webb, both the L.C.C. and the board of education agreed to commit to major public funding for the new institution on condition that private funding was secured.[21] At this point Haldane and Webb publicly announced the

---

[17] C. W. Boyd, 'Beit, Alfred (1853–1906)', in *O.D.N.B.* <https://doi.org/10.1093/ref:odnb/30676> [accessed 30 May 2018].

[18] They supported his Hospital Fund, launched when he was still prince of Wales in 1897 to which Wernher eventually left a bequest of £390,000, and Alfred and Otto Beit over £125,000 (F. K. Prochaska, *Philanthropy and the Hospitals of London: the King's Fund, 1897–1990* (Oxford, 1992), p. 30–1).

[19] Ashby and Anderson, *Portrait of Haldane at Work*, p. 51.

[20] Extract from *The Times,* 10 July 1908, contained in Imperial College Archives, Bessemer Memorial Fund and Bessemer Laboratory, correspondence, 1903–15, HD/4/1.

[21] A. R. Hall, *Science for Industry: a Short History of the Imperial College of Science and Technology* (1982), p. 31. See also *The Diary of Beatrice Webb, ii: 1892–1905*, ed. N. Mackenzie and J. Mackenzie (Cambridge, Mass, 1983 edn.), entry for 23 July 1903.

magnificent pledge of £100,000 cash from Wernher, Beit & Co. towards the new technical college.[22] This involved establishing a trust to oversee the disbursement of the donation, chaired by Lord Rosebery and including Wernher, Haldane, Balfour, Sir Francis Mowatt (joint permanent secretary to the treasury) and the duke of Devonshire.

This was still four years before the establishment of Imperial College – a period during which leading individuals involved with relevant institutions, including Mowatt from the treasury (who suggested including 'Imperial' in the name) and Sir Robert Morant, permanent secretary at the board of education, mooted the idea of a merger between the City and Guilds College, the R.C.S. and the R.S.M., poring over the nature of these three component parts, their relationship with the developing University of London, and the acquisition of real estate and money. Haldane was able to play a pivotal role in the discussion and negotiation, being appointed in 1904 chairman of an official departmental committee on the Royal College of Science, whose members included Webb and Wernher, and whose remit included investigation of the whole South Kensington complex (including the R.S.M.).[23] The 'Minutes of Evidence' provide a very full background to the whole history of the three bodies that came to form the new collegiate institution, besides an analysis of technical education in competitor countries, and throw particular light on problems in the education and training of those in the mining industry. Reporting in 1906, the committee endorsed annual central and local government support of £40,000 (half each from the treasury and the L.C.C.); confirmed that the 1851 commissioners had agreed to give the remainder of their estate to the new institution; announced the agreement of the Council of the City and Guilds of London Institute to enter the scheme; and set out detailed recommendations for the institution's governing structure.[24] The following year the Imperial College of Science and Technology was formally incorporated, with characteristic Edwardian pomp and fanfare, its Charter declaring its prime object to be:

---

[22] It is not entirely clear whether this pledge was directed specifically to the R.S.M. aspect of the new project, but this was where the bulk of their pledge went. Fundraising for the Bessemer Memorial Fund was publicly associated with the Wernher, Beit & Co. donation.

[23] The original chairman, Mowatt, had to stand down through illness. The official centenary historian of Imperial College challenges the importance given to Haldane (by Ashby and Andersen) in its original creation (H. Gay, *History of Imperial College London 1907–2007: Higher Education and Research in Science, Technology and Medicine* (2007), p. 64, n. 17). But there is no denying the facts of his membership of key bodies involved, of his ongoing involvement in the development of the University of London over several decades, nor of his relevant ideological thinking.

[24] *Departmental Report on the Royal College of Science, Final Report* (Parliamentary Papers 1906 [Cd.2872] xxxi), pp. 391–429.

the establishment at South Kensington of an institution or group of associated Colleges, of Science and Technology, where the highest specialised instruction should be given, and where the fullest equipment for ... training and research should be provided in various branches of sciences, especially in its application to industry for which no sufficient provision already exists elsewhere.[25]

At the time Imperial College did not become part of the University of London. It was, effectively, a federation of three institutions within which the City and Guilds Institute fought hard to maintain a certain amount of autonomy in terms of finance and teaching.[26]

Beit was not present at the 1907 inaugural ceremony. Always physically weak, he had died the previous year at his country home in Hertfordshire, unmarried, aged fifty-three. His immense wealth benefited three significant areas of his life. Towards the Imperial College project he bequeathed £50,000 plus 5,000 preference shares (valued at some £85,000) in De Beers Consolidated Mines Ltd. He was also generous to leading medical causes including the King Edward VII Hospital Fund. To his native city of Hamburg, with which he had remained involved, he left generous contributions towards social and philanthropic institutions. But the bulk of his huge legacy went to southern Africa where his heart lay: this included £200,000 divided among the newly founded university in Cape Town, funding for Rhodes University in Grahamstown, and other educational and charitable purposes. The lion's share – £1.2 million – was designated for the expansion of communication networks throughout southern Africa. This became the Beit Trust.[27]

The Beit-Wernher link with the new Imperial College of Science and Technology was continued through the involvement of Wernher and then, very actively, of Otto Beit (Alfred's brother). Shortly after its establishment Wernher joined the Imperial College Mining and Metallurgy Committee and four years later was awarded the gold medal of the Institution of Mining and Metallurgy 'for his personal services to the advancement of technical education'.[28] He died in 1912 and was generous to many of the same causes as his former friend and colleague, Alfred Beit – notably educational institutions. This included £250,000 to what became the University of Cape Town. To

[25] Charter of Imperial College of Science and Technology, 1907.,

[26] For further detail see Hall, *Science for Industry*, p. 36. It was not until 1929 that it formally became part of the University of London.

[27] H. Albrecht, *Alfred Beit: the Hamburg Diamond King* (Hamburg, 2007, English transl. 2012), p. 122. Otto Beit and Julius Wernher were two of the trustees of the Beit Trust. See also Trevelyan, *Grand Dukes and Diamonds*, p. 191.

[28] F. E. Douglas, Board of Education to Julius Wernher, 18 Oct. 1907; Julius Wernher to F. E. Douglas, 22 Oct. 1907 (Imperial College archives, Wernher Correspondence, 1907–14, B/WER/1, no. 79). See also Colvin, 'Wernher, Sir Julius Charles'.

Imperial College Wernher left £150,000, plus part of his residuary estate, amounting to £45,000.[29]

In 1909 the new rector of Imperial College proudly invited Otto Beit to call on the architect, Aston Webb, to inspect plans for what promised to be 'one of the best buildings, if not *the* best building, in the world'.[30] It was the new R.S.M. complex, erected between 1909 and 1913 in Prince Consort Road. Built of Portland stone, the imposing facade sent out strong signals of the majesty of empire.[31] Its vast, three-storey high semicircular central niche was flanked by imposing monuments on either side, designed by P. R. Montford, to commemorate Alfred Beit and Julius Wernher whose busts remain today atop Renaissance-style pedestals. It is hard to judge whether these statues were erected to honour the benefactions of these two individuals or, in addition, to celebrate what they represented in terms of colonialism and empire. What is certain is that their benefactions to the new institution, in particular, to the R.S.M., were extremely important in the project's fruition. An interesting document in the Imperial College archives lists sources of non-recurrent funding for the new institution between 1909 and 1919 (including from government departments and the cost of land granted). This shows that the combination of individual private donations and legacies, dominated by those of Beit and Wernher, amounted to some 34 per cent of the total figure of £1,269,774.[32]

Otto Beit's connections, interests and racial prejudices strongly echo those of his brother to whom he was close. His fortune derived from his major shareholding in Wernher, Beit & Co. and its successor (from 1905), the Central Mining and Investment Corporation Ltd. He too was an admirer of Rhodes and his plans for colonial expansion, and he and Wernher were nominated trustees of the Beit Trust. While bound up with Rand society, partly through his marriage to the daughter of a local mining engineer, like Alfred he acquired British citizenship and settled in London, living a fashionable life in Mayfair, becoming a renowned picture collector and philanthropist. After the death of his brother he devoted his working life to administering the Beit Trust and its objectives.[33] Between 1909 and his death in 1930 he was closely associated with

---

[29] The *O.D.N.B.* entry for Wernher states that he had endowed Imperial College with £250,000 at an earlier stage.

[30] Rector to Otto Beit, 9 Jul. 1909 (Imperial College archives, B/Beit/1/1).

[31] Roy MacLeod points out that, in fact, Webb's façade was 'merely a front' for 'an assortment of poorly designed laboratories' (R. Macleod, '"Instructed men" and mining engineers: the associates of the Royal School of Mines and British Imperial Science, 1851–1920', *Minerva*, xxxii (1994), 73).

[32] 'List of Donations, Legacies, etc., from the opening of the College to 31st December 1919', undated document (Imperial College archives, Sir Otto Beit papers, B/Beit/1/1).

[33] It was Otto Beit who was largely responsible for a major bridge-building programme,

Figure 4.1. Statues of Julius Wernher (L) and Alfred Beit (R), by Paul R Montford, erected 1910, at the entrance to the former Royal School of Mines, part of Imperial College of Science and Technology. It is conjectured that the strange allegorical figures under the busts – including the figure apparently digging – may commemorate the combination of imperialism and European mining interests of Cecil Rhodes and his two allies in southern Africa represented here. See George P. Landow, <www.victorianweb.org/sculpture/montford/7.html> [accessed 1 May 2018]. Photograph: Philippa Lewis.

Imperial College, taking an interest in its activities and regularly providing financial support. Its whole ethos at that time would have chimed with his sympathies. The rector (1910–22), Sir Alfred Keogh, a near contemporary, had seen distinguished service in southern Africa as a senior army medical officer during the Boer War. The chairman of the governing body (of which Beit was a loyal member between 1912 and 1930, and, for a while, chair of its finance committee) was Lord Crewe, a Liberal cabinet minister with imperial experience in Asquith's cabinet as colonial secretary and then secretary for India. Serving the 'far corners of the Empire', something dear to Beit's heart in connection with southern Africa, had been part of the tradition of each of the three constituent colleges of Imperial College – particularly of the R.S.M. – and its governing body 'saw it as its duty that this pattern be maintained'.[34] As a pillar of the Establishment, Otto Beit was rewarded with a knighthood in 1920 and a baronetcy in 1924. He too was extremely generous to Imperial College not only in his lifetime but through his legacy. Among other bequests he left £26,000 for the endowment of Beit Fellowships for Scientific Research, tenable at Imperial College and 'open to men and women of European descent by both parents, but otherwise of any nationality whatever'.[35]

So, how were those two figures atop their pedestals at the entry to the R.S.M. judged in their time as symbols of imperial wealth and power? Were Wernher and Beit colonial buccaneers who, having exploited people and resources in the British empire for their private gain, settled in its capital where they flaunted their wealth and pushed their way into high society through their philanthropy? Views of this kind emerged particularly during the 1897 parliamentary committee of inquiry into the Jameson Raid when Beit was vigorously attacked by Sir William Harcourt and Henry Labouchère. Radical public figures, including Hilaire Belloc, the labour leader John Burns and the political theorist J. A. Hobson were vociferous in their criticism of the 'Randlords' and their world. Hobson's polemic against imperialism and the Boer War gave a vivid account of the iniquities of the labour policy of the Transvaal mine-owners, describing the so-called 'location system' which tied workers to the mines for life in semi-slavery conditions without any bargaining power over their wages.[36] (Yet Hobson made clear his own racist prejudices in denouncing the Boer War as 'a Jewish war'.[37])

---

part of which was the Beit Memorial Bridge (1929) over the Limpopo river, linking South Africa with what was then Rhodesia.

[34] Gay, *History of Imperial College London*, p. 202.

[35] Lord Buckmaster (chairman of the governing body of Imperial College of Science and Technology), letter to *The Times*, 11 December 1930, p. 12.

[36] J. A. Hobson, *Imperialism: a Study* (1902), p. 302.

[37] J. A. Hobson, *The War in South Africa: its Causes and Effects* (1900); D. Feldman, 'Jews

A counterview of these rich, foreign newcomers seems to have been more current: that they were creative and highly successful entrepreneurs, skilled in and passionate about their business and about the development of the part of the world in which they operated. They had settled in congenial London high society and engaged in a project that addressed their concern about England's lack of technological skills – particularly in mining techniques. Both Wernher and the Beit brothers (and, indeed, Rhodes) all held a strong belief in the importance of education and used their wealth in many ways to promote educational institutions in South Africa and Germany as well as England. Wernher was allegedly 'deeply concerned at the backwardness of his adopted country in practical science'.[38] Beit well understood the crying need for better-educated mining engineers particularly to go out and exploit colonial opportunities. The new Imperial College of Science and Technology, and in particular its Royal School of Mines, was a highly appropriate focus for their philanthropy. Between its formal opening and the outbreak of war in 1914 major developments were made in important new areas of applied science.[39] At the R.S.M., by 1911 the Bessemer Laboratory for metallurgy was in place as a critical element in its teaching and research. For Associates of the R.S.M. 'the world was their oyster' as a result of Europe's expanding economies which needed 'vast quantities of minerals'. Substantial numbers worked in North and South America, Africa, Australia and Asia, without doubt promoting 'the pace and nature of colonial economic growth'.[40]

Today, the Aston Webb R.S.M. building in Prince Consort Road, with its imposing commemorative busts, is a period piece: the only remaining building of Imperial College that dates back to imperial days. There is no question that the two men commemorated there were significant in the founding of that institution. Whether they were honoured on an imperial building as symbols not just of generous donors but also as 'imperialists' – something that does not resonate well today – and therefore deserve to be considered for removal, is beyond the scope of this essay which aims to explain the origins of their wealth, the motives behind their benefactions and the context of the society in which they made those major donations.

---

and the British empire *c.*1900', *History Workshop Jour.*, lxiii (2007), 70–80, at p. 75ff.

[38] Colvin, 'Wernher, Sir Julius Charles'.

[39] These included plant physiology, aeronautics, chemical technology, biochemistry and cytology (Hall, *Science for Industry*, pp. 44ff).

[40] MacLeod, '"Instructed men"', pp. 432, 434.

5. The expectations of benefactors and a responsibility to endow

John Shakeshaft

Let me begin, if I may, with a paradox in lieu of a question. Universities, and particularly Cambridge to whose behaviours I shall refer in this essay, seek the benefactions of accumulated wealth to pursue ideas, teach and publish freely for the public good without private benefit. To give, and not to count the cost, perhaps. I shall argue as Augustine did in his late sermons – this is a famously persistent concern for scholars – that seeking wealth to endow, sustain and manage the institutions of the University is for the benefit of the many and an enduring responsibility.[1] Pursuing, considering and receiving benefaction engages Cambridge with its social purpose.

If we turn from the lineage of discovery and the description of scholarly benefaction in the fragilities of fourth-century north Africa to the early nineteenth century, the German savant and natural scientist, Alexander von Humboldt commented at the foundation of the University of Berlin in 1810 that 'the richest universities are those where sciences enjoy the deepest and most mindful treatment'. He had in mind Cambridge and Oxford, even in their unreformed state before the onset of state-directed change in the mid nineteenth century. Humboldt believed, however, that wealth alone would not produce excellence; that, he thought was a matter of ethic.[2] Universities were to be engaged with the proprieties of their own times, including in their management of their finances, as we still are.

Private benefaction is vital to the University of Cambridge and its colleges in several different contexts – in ethical, civic or public engagement, in the broadening and dissemination of science and knowledge, as well as financially in sustaining endowments for income and security. A fifth of

---

[1] See P. Brown, *Through the Eye of a Needle: Wealth, the Fall of Rome and the Making of Christianity in the West, 350–550 AD* (Princeton, N.J., 2012), pp. 347–52; P. Brown, *Ransom of the Soul* (Cambridge, Mass., 2015).

[2] See C. Wellmon, *Organizing Enlightenment: Information Overload and the Invention of the Modern Research University* (Baltimore, Md., 2015), pp. 210–20; Wellmon's enquiries into concepts of university organization in the Enlightenment were stimulated by contemporary concerns about the pursuit of funds and academic freedom at the University of Virginia.

J. Shakeshaft, 'The expectations of benefactors and a responsibility to endow', in *Dethroning historical reputations: universities, museums and the commemoration of benefactors*, ed. J. Pellew and L. Goldman (2018), pp. 47–55.

Cambridge's academic income comes from the yield on endowment and a slightly higher proportion of capital expenditure is directly endowed.[3] Endowment is itself purposeful wealth. Responsibility for its management and use, and the ideas which inform it, are accountably those of the University as discovered and developed over time and in due process. We seek, receive and acknowledge benefactors and their gifts as nearly as we can in accordance with our stated ethics.[4]

Private and public benefactions have been essential to the University since its foundation; indeed, they help describe the purposes of the corporation. Understanding the nature of the relationship and the expectations of donors, and 'describing' the University and its personnel with possible projects in perspective, helps to determine both the appropriateness of the funds, gifts and benefactions solicited and the value of our teaching and scholarship. Until its reformulation into a regulator under the 2017 Higher Education Act, the Higher Education Funding Council for England (H.E.F.C.E.) was, like the Arts Council established after the Second World War, an effective patron-benefactor of universities.[5] It was an important and respected source of funds with well-articulated expectations of performance and assessment rather than regulatory requirements, which allowed the University to describe and account for itself within discovered and constantly questioned purposes. H.E.F.C.E. provided a component of Cambridge's necessarily diversified finances and also respected, in our case, the importance and peculiarities of self-governance.[6]

The diversity of expectations of donors, funders and benefactors can only be reconciled if the University has well-articulated, responsive and developing views of its purposes, and the solicitation, receipt and stewardship of funds can be measured and accounted in due process against such values, finance and association. Recent examples might be the gifts of more than £100

---

[3] 'Report and financial statements for the year ended 31 July 2017', *Cambridge University Reporter*, no. 6489, 14 Dec. 2017 <https://www.admin.cam.ac.uk/reporter/2017-18/weekly/6489/section4.shtml> [accessed 26 March 2018].

[4] See 'The university's mission and core values' <http://www.cam.ac.uk/about-the-university/how-the-university-and-colleges-work/the-universitys-mission-and-core-values> [accessed 26 March 2018].

[5] 'Annual report of the general board to the council', *Cambridge University Reporter*, no. 6489, 14 Dec. 2017 <https://www.admin.cam.ac.uk/reporter/2017-18/weekly/6489/section3.shtml> [accessed 26 March 2018].

[6] See 'Memorandum of assurance and accountability between HEFCE and institutions' <http://www.hefce.ac.uk/pubs/year/2016/201612/> [accessed 26 March 2018]; University of Cambridge, *Council Handbook 2015*, ch. 1, 'Role of council and the duties and responsibilities of members' <https://www.governance.cam.ac.uk/committees/council/handbook-2015/Pages/Duties-and-responsibilities.aspx> [accessed 26 March 2018].

million from the Dolby family and foundation for fundamental research and teaching in physics, scientific buildings and a college court, which recognizes thereby the whole civic context of scholarship.[7] Or we might point to the gifts of even greater amounts from the Sainsbury family, and other foundations and trusts, similarly directed to the entire purpose of scholarly science, particularly in biology.[8] These gifts, and many comparable donations, are comprehensive in their generosity and thereby support the life of the whole corporate University.

But let us take a different and perhaps controversial example. Tuition fees are priced neither by the cost of the service offered nor by the market demand of students, but rather by political determination of certain expected social inputs and outcomes. They are the inverse of private benefactions. Were it not for its diverse sources of funds from outside the public sector, Collegiate Cambridge would be unable to subsidize the cost of undergraduate education to the tune of approximately 45 per cent or £8,000 per student.[9] The relationship of the University, as a public good, with the British state is historically complex. Were the expectations of a particular private benefactor or public authority to become determinative, contrary to the open purposes of the place, teaching and scholarship could themselves be impaired.

The value and importance of diversified funding and its congruence with the mission and purposes of the University is also reflected in commercial enterprise. Cambridge University Press and Cambridge Assessment, for example, are integral parts of the University, contributing to its commitment to educate, and generating the funds to do so.[10] The University manages its endowment through the Cambridge University Endowment Fund; the quality of its subscription, process and engagement with external managers who look after the funds, and the university's openness and accountability in the stewardship of them, should also be seen to reflect the mission of the

---

[7] The Dolby gift is described at <http://www.cam.ac.uk/research/news/ps85-million-gift-from-the-dolby-family-to-transform-cambridge-science> [accessed 26 March 2018].

[8] See references to the Sainsbury family at <http://www.philanthropy.cam.ac.uk> [accessed 26 March 2018].

[9] The university cost of educating an undergraduate is approximately £17,000 p.a.; tuition fees for home and E.U. students cover £9,250. Total external research funding covers approximately 70% of the actual costs (see annual efficiency return, value for money report and annual accountability return to H.E.F.C.E. for 2016–7, *Cambridge University Reporter*, forthcoming).

[10] 2016/17 annual reports of Cambridge Assessment <http://www.cambridgeassessment.org.uk/Images/463822-annual-review-16-17.pdf> and Cambridge University Press <http://www.cambridge.org/about-us/who-we-are/annual-report> [both accessed 26 March 2018].

University itself.[11] We rehearse these expectations annually in our attestable statement of investment responsibility itself, and our subjection to audit and scrutiny.[12]

More challenging, perhaps, is to raise or accept funding, principally for research but also for buildings, where there is an expectation of express outcome, or of a particular product, either in the solicitation and proposition of funds or in the gift of the benefactor. Where this takes a particular form and often raises concern is in the establishment of named institutes where directed public policy prescriptions and recommendations derive from research. Separating the concern, fascination and engagement of a benefactor with the purposes of the institute from the promotion of a sectional interest, intentional or not, is a constant task. In the fields of energy and climate change research, the maintenance of appropriate, acknowledged and valued relationships with external sponsors, in highly charged areas of public policy, is a good and robust example of the challenges faced and also met by the University.[13] Promoting ideas and policy from evidence without misleading or being misled has to be the University's aim, and it informs all our external engagements.[14]

In our latest funding campaign, *'Dear World ... Yours, Cambridge'*, for example, we describe the worldliness of our scholarly aspirations for benefaction as causes: ideas, institutions and lines of enquiry that individuals and trusts might wish to understand, support and encourage with or without public recognition.[15] With teaching and the dissemination of ideas so integral to our purposes, and with academic self-government our constitution, not to mention the responsibility which inheres in a scholar's tenured freedom to enquire and express, and the right he or she possesses to retain intellectual property, academics in Cambridge are encouraged, tutored and administratively supported to take the lead in seeking benefaction and engaging with donors.[16] And yet – another reference to

---

[11] Cambridge University Endowment Fund, Investment Management report 30 June 2017, information made available privately to the author.

[12] Report of the Working Group on Investment Responsibility, 13 June 2016 available in *Cambridge University Reporter* <http://www.admin.cam.ac.uk/reporter/2015-16/weekly/6430/section1.shtml#heading2-5> [accessed 26 March 2018].

[13] Discussions of the University's Divestment Working Group, information made available privately to the author.

[14] This is recognized in the annual reports of the Risk Steering Committee (information made available privately to the author). Mitigated by A.C.B.E.L.A. diligence and Brand Licensing.

[15] The campaign for the university and colleges of Cambridge <https://www.philanthropy.cam.ac.uk> [accessed 26 March 2018].

[16] <https://www.philanthropy.cam.ac.uk> [accessed 26 March 2018] and internal guidance.

fourth century debates between Augustine and Leporius might be in order here[17] – it is crucial not to tie research to a particular donor or their wishes. Paradoxically, the absence of this type of formal requirement, permitting freedom of enquiry within research, often leads to greater fulfilment of expectations and even utility. We have, as I mentioned earlier, fine and current examples of minerals research, climate change and environmental policy in Cambridge where the apparent and immediate corporate interests of the donor have seemed at variance with the possible results of research into energy alternatives, and yet the freedom of enquiry has yielded useful, applicable science and policy change.[18] We also have recent cases of different domestic and external political controversies in area studies where certain appointments – and particularly the published research – have seemed inimical to the shorter-term interests or reputation of the benefactor who has given willingly. One of the enduring reasons why we seek to know our benefactors well, the requirements of the law apart, is to be assured that they appreciate that their expectations may not be fulfilled and that they involve themselves disinterestedly without expecting a hoped-for prescription.[19]

Priorities for causes are established within the ethic of the University itself. Schools, faculties and departments promote scholarly themes; the General Board, the academic governor of the University, endorses and disseminates areas of expected discovery; initiative at the beginning and end belongs to scholars and their academic teams. The University mediates through administrative support, development, finance and the oversight of multiple external partnerships. There should be no purposeless targeting of wealth or capital for its own sake. Rather, we hope that every approach and proposal for benefaction is based on a genuine academic need and resonates with the interests and intentions of the donor. The development and nurturing of relationships is at the core of our funding, co-ordinated across all possible sources of income and gift, and informs the responsibility assumed. Our current process for solicitation, approval and acceptance of donations, indeed all substantial external engagements of the University affecting reputation and mission, is known by the acronym A.C.B.E.L.A., Advisory Committee on Benefactions and External Legal Engagements. It was established after an institution-wide enquiry led by the University's Council, the executive body, into political relationships, gifts, naming and corporate integrity. A.C.B.E.L.A is a non-adversarial means of assessing and endorsing engagement through which the Council as trustees can discharge

---

[17] Brown, *Through the Eye of a Needle*, p. 484.

[18] This is currently applicable notably in life sciences, area studies and earth sciences.

[19] See Board of Scrutiny description, role and reports <http://www.scrutiny.cam.ac.uk> [accessed 26 March 2018].

its responsibility openly and knowledgeably.[20] We compete for money as indeed we do internationally for students, scholars and professors as well. Competition helps define value, purpose and engagement with our peers in Europe, Asia and North America; it also influences whom we approach and how we conduct ourselves with partners.

Given the diversity and administrative complexity of a collegiate university composed of many institutions and myriad independent thinkers and teachers with multiple corporate, commercial and institutional relationships, I had wanted to avoid the overworked analogy of an 'eco-system' until I read in the same essay quoted earlier that Humboldt himself had used the term to describe the organic and fruitful relationship between faculties in Berlin some seventy years before the construction of modern Cambridge.[21] We and our benefactors belong to an eco-system; perhaps that is the nature of a collegiate university with multiple faculties; the human geography matters. That leads in acknowledging relationships and recognizing what is an appropriate association – and if it cannot be acknowledged and recognized within occasional bounds of discretion it is unlikely to be appropriate – to attempting in a difficult and yet vital aspect of competition to define, describe and assess the changing narrative of reputation, the brand.

The common culture of expectation within the University is of excellence in teaching, research and enquiry.[22] However, there are multiple perceptions of its behaviours, as well as the external assessment of the University's research, publications and now teaching, meaning that our reputation is always fragile, vulnerable and inherently unmanageable. We know that there is great value placed by donors and business partners on public association with Cambridge; we would hope that we are in turn enhanced by our donors and associates; the brand is renewed and affected by our partnerships and public connections. The memorials of association change over time, affording insight into what was once held to be significant: the histories of the commission and hanging of portraits, the acceptance and placing of busts, and the funding and naming of buildings – whether planned or, more frequently, not – would certainly illuminate the University's evolving views of itself. But the University is not a garden of remembrance. Each name, each gift, each memorial has to be accounted with the living purposes of

[20] University of Cambridge, *Council Handbook 2017* <https://www.governance.cam.ac.uk/committees/council/handbook-2017/Pages/default.aspx> and *Strategic Agreements* <http://www.strategic-partnerships.admin.cam.ac.uk/strategic-agreements> [both accessed 26 March 2018].

[21] Wellmon, *Organizing Enlightenment*, p. 228.

[22] See the university mission statement referenced at n. 4 above.

the place. In retrospect, there are often once-lauded ideas and individuals whose standing, reputation and behaviour assume different and usually uncomfortable contemporary significance. Here I might instance Jan Christian Smuts, military leader, member of British war cabinets, second prime minister of South Africa, segregationist and former chancellor of the University, whose busts and former portraits have now been removed from prominent places.[23]

We have no formal means of expulsion from the pantheon.[24] To do so would be to censure our own history, though over time the deemed appropriateness of some relationships changes. Tobacco, widely consumed for pleasure nonetheless, is an uncontroversial example.[25] Practically though, how do we seek to ensure that our external relations and engagements, including commercial pursuits, maintain and reflect the integrity or expectations of the University and especially its students? The University is a self-governing corporation; its trustees and directors, the members of Council, are bound by law, inclination and regulation to act in its best interests and to be accountable for having done so. We are responsible for the external relationships we enjoy. We determine the appropriateness to the University of soliciting and accepting particular benefactions, donors and external relationships more broadly in the regular, established, consultative and advisory process that is A.C.B.E.L.A.[26] The process itself is also regularly scrutinized and reported through the University's audit committee's annual reports. If there is a particular area of concern to the University – the nature of responsible investment, for example – we establish competent working groups to hear and analyse evidence openly and to report with policy recommendations to Council.[27] Within A.C.B.E.L.A. we examine the terms

[23] A portrait of J. C. Smuts, chancellor of the university *1948–50*, has been removed from the hall of his college, Christ's, and his bust from the Old Schools. Less savoury university dignitaries remain.

[24] 'Naming policy for buildings and spaces in buildings', 2017 (information made available privately to the author).

[25] 'Cambridge University adopts Cancer Research UK guidelines on involvement with tobacco industries and investments', see *Cancer Research UK* <http://www.universitiesuk. ac.uk/policy-and-analysis/reports/Pages/tobacco-industry-funding-to-universities> [accessed 26 March 2018].

[26] University of Cambridge annual report for the academic year 2012–13, esp. p. 5, 'Woolf Inquiry Report: Audit Committee Working Group' <https://www.cam.ac.uk/system/files/ reports_and_financial_statements_for_the_year_ended_31_july_2013.pdf> [accessed 26 March 2018].

[27] See University's Divestment Working Group <https://www.governance.cam.ac.uk/ committees/divestment-wg/Pages/default.aspx> [accessed 26 March 2018] and reports of its discussions in *Cambridge University Reporter* <https://www.reporter.admin.cam.ac.uk> [accessed 26 March 2018].

of an engagement, the expectations on both sides and the limits of control, as well as considering the public acknowledgement of gifts, the recognition of benefactors and the variety of memorials involved, from named buildings to statues, busts and portraits of both the living and the dead.[28] We seek to ensure and be assured that the acceptance of any gift or the solicitation of funding is procedurally, legally and demonstrably distinct from offers of admission to the University, the conduct of teaching and research, and the award of degrees. Indeed, this diligence was a consideration in the report advocating the establishment of A.C.B.E.L.A.[29]

There are, of course, real challenges to the process and to our decisions, born of changing perceptions of 'appropriateness' and the changing value placed on certain research or ideas. Equally challenging within an historic community of scholars with changing ideas and sometimes *un*common behaviours, is sustaining and recognizing free enquiry and expression in the institution in the past as well as present. What we choose to affirm in our past, and the greats with whom we might want to be associated, will always be a reflection of our present concerns for the future; understanding these often determines the appropriateness of action, particularly with regard to memorials. We need, therefore, and have instituted a process of self-examination and transparency in the acceptance of gifts in order for trustees to be assured that they have acted in the best interests of the University and sought to maintain the integrity of the diverse place itself.[30]

In assessing donations, we strive to understand the history of the donor and the context of the benefaction; we consult widely. Certain strictures are given by law, the Modern Slavery and the Anti-Bribery and Corruption Acts for example, which require evident diligence or so-called adequate procedures. Typically, within the University, a senior member would be expected to be responsible for a relationship with a donor; blind reception of a benefaction is now essentially inappropriate. International practice, regarding sanctioned or politically engaged persons, must also be considered, as must be the formal prejudice of association with other sources of funds: tobacco corporations and the subsequent objection of Cancer Research U.K. is perhaps the best known case in Cambridge's recent history.[31] However,

[28] 'Naming policy for buildings and spaces in buildings', 2017 (information made available privately to the author).

[29] 'Woolf inquiry report: audit committee working group' (see n. 26 above).

[30] University of Cambridge, *Council Handbook 2017* <https://www.governance.cam.ac.uk/committees/council/handbook-2017/Pages/Duties-and-responsibilities.aspx> [accessed 26 March 2018].

[31] 'Cancer Research UK code of practice on tobacco industry funding to universities', *Cancer Research UK* <http://www.cancerresearchuk.org/funding-for-researchers/applying-

understanding what is specifically prejudicial or indeed beneficial is always more nuanced and complex than the more common questions relating to the public value of association with a particular corporation, activity or person.[32] We also have to consider the proposed form of association: sometimes corporate, sometimes continuous funding, sometimes a single donation, sometimes eleemosynary, consultative and collaborative. To the extent possible, we use the resources of the University itself, separate from the beneficiaries of a donation, to achieve an understanding of the nuances surrounding particular engagements to determine what is and is not appropriate. This has been notably effective in maintaining and developing valuable partnerships in otherwise sanctioned or politically difficult territories on a transparent basis.

So much for the pursuit of benefactions and the managing of relationships in the best interests of the University. I should note that we are also responsible investors, stewards of these donations. Our periodically assessed statement of investment responsibility essentially says that Cambridge will seek to invest and engage with managers who accountably espouse the values expressed by the University. Scrutiny, accountability and process discover and describe those values, which necessarily change over time. As such, there is no proscription on investment, rather a prescription of engagement and espousal of expected values. By constant assessment and occasional mistakes, we pursue the mission.

I might conclude with Augustine. The responsibility to endow is a public good. Therefore, we must understand our benefactors.

---

for-funding/policies-that-affect-your-grant/code-of-practice-on-tobacco-industry-funding-to-universities> [accessed 28 Feb. 2018].

[32] Diligence is conducted by A.C.B.E.L.A. principally through the University of Cambridge, department of Development and Alumni Relations (C.U.D.A.R.), sponsors and third parties.

6. The funder's perspective

Victoria Harrison

On the basis of varied experience in different types of fundraising, I will discuss four questions in this essay: how far should the origin of funds be scrutinized and publicized; what are the benefactors' motives and expectations; how far can and should benefactors have influence; and how far are the founders constrained by the structures that grow out of their pioneering effort?[1] In considering these questions, I will give special attention to the issue of 'naming' because of its overall relevance.

On the first question, funding by government presents relatively few problems. The research councils, for example, readily assign their institutes and laboratories titles such as the 'M.R.C. Laboratory of Molecular Biology', the 'M.R.C. Biostatistics Unit', or the 'B.B.S.R.C. Bioenergy Centre'. They were not only set up with funds assumed to be 'respectable', but could be closed if circumstances changed and if no longer needed. The names of prominent and relevant researchers are sometimes incorporated uncontroversially into the title of such institutions: the 'M.R.C. Weatherall Institute' or the 'Sanger Institute', for example. Royal Society or British Academy professorships (government funded and for a limited term) also seem acceptable.

The frontier between public and private funding is not, however, clear-cut. To begin with, public funding can come from municipal institutions as well

---

[1] My perspective reflects a career within three types of funding body. First, in funding by government from within three research councils: the Medical Research Council [M.R.C.] from 1971 to 1989 (interspersed with a secondment to the Cabinet Office dealing with science policy), the Agriculture and Food Research Council [A.F.R.C.] from 1989 to 1994 and the Biotechnology and Biological Sciences Research Council [B.B.S.R.C.] from 1994 to 1997. Here my roles included operating the peer-review system whereby funds were allocated to universities and research institutes and progress was monitored and assessed. Next came nine years in a charitable foundation as chief executive in the Wolfson Foundation from 1997 to 2006, administering grants made mainly for capital projects in universities, museums and galleries, historic buildings and schools. Last came my role as a trustee within a charity that supports institutions primarily funded by government: as a trustee from 2007 to 2017 of the University College London Hospital [U.C.L.H.] Charity, which in my last two years I have chaired. Since 2011 I have also been a trustee for an independent special-needs charity, Hearing Dogs for Deaf People, where we seek funds rather than distribute them.

V. Harrison, 'The funder's perspective', in *Dethroning historical reputations: universities, museums and the commemoration of benefactors*, ed. J. Pellew and L. Goldman (2018), pp. 57–63.

as from central government; many nineteenth-century British universities, for example, owed less to central government initiative than to the municipal pride of great provincial cities: Liverpool to William Rathbone, for example; Birmingham to Joseph Chamberlain. British universities can also combine acceptance of public funding with incorporating a major benefactor into their title: Aberdeen's Robert Gordon University, for example, or Liverpool John Moores University (as renamed from 1992), not to mention major institutions within a university such as Oxford University's Nuffield, Kellogg and Wolfson colleges.

'Naming' difficulties do not seem to arise with charities that lack the name of an individual. The University College London Hospital charity, for instance, likes its grants to be acknowledged, partly as a way to advertise its existence and thus ensure an ongoing flow of funds through legacies and donations. With 'naming' after individuals, though, it may sometimes seem wise to hesitate – as with investments – where (for example) slavery, tobacco or armaments manufacture are involved. Universities are increasingly setting up committees to adjudicate on these issues, and their minutes, when released, may provide rich sources for future historians. I do, however, know that some academics think that charitable funds when transferred to a university are thereby washed whiter than white.

But what of private benefactors' motives and expectations? Richard Crossman, Labour M.P. and minister, reacting strongly in 1973 against the inter-war labour movement's repudiation of charity, claimed that 'if volunteering is stifled, the altruistic motive which exists in normal people is blocked or perverted with deplorable results on the community'.[2] He was pioneering a shift in opinion that by the end of the century lay at the heart of 'New Labour'. In the Goodman lecture (2000) Gordon Brown said that 'those who embark on voluntary action out of a sense of duty often end up with the realisation that it has brought a new richness of meaning to their own lives – that in the giving, they have received in a different way as well'.[3] As with any human activity, charitable motives will be numerous, interacting and complex. They may include a desire to promote a particular area of study that interests the donor, or a cure for a disease from which donors or their relatives have suffered. The search for a cure for the child that dies young, a motive now diminishing, still remains significant – in the Anthony Nolan Trust, for example, set up in 1980 by his mother to create a bone-marrow transplant register which might have enabled her son

[2] R. H. S. Crossman, *The Role of the Volunteer in the Modern Social Service* (Sidney Ball Memorial Lecture 1973, Oxford, 1973), p. 21.

[3] G. Brown, *Civic Society in Modern Britain* (17th Arnold Goodman lecture, 2001), p. 26; see <http://www.hm-treasury.gov.uk/speeches.htm> [accessed 16 Apr. 2018].

to survive. There may be a wish to promote a particular cause, such as the Wolfson Foundation's funding of buildings in all the Oxbridge women's colleges in the 1960s to promote women's education. A benefaction may result from a desire to perpetuate gratitude to the source of the benefactors' personal success, such as the university which educated them. The incentive may arise from the aspiration of the newly rich or of an ethnic minority to win social acceptance: it was a shrewd move on both sides when the prince of Wales in 1990, at a reception, invited rich Asian businessmen to support his Youth Business Trust, to which they responded generously, so that by the time coffee had been served, £5 million had been raised.[4] Another motive may be a sense of guilt at survival. Numerous statues, gardens and buildings in Britain as well as war memorials reflect the huge philanthropic impact made by two world wars. Dame Stephanie Shirley's outlook illuminates the close relationship between entrepreneurship, philanthropy, and gratitude to the society that enabled her to survive. Referring to her status as an unaccompanied child refugee arriving in the U.K., she explains that 'there is a relationship between trauma and entrepreneurship. You become a survivor, full-stop. I think my "guilt" about surviving the Holocaust gave me a strong urge to prove my life had been worth saving', and she saw philanthropy as 'a kind of contract', that 'you get as much as you give. The more I give away, the richer I feel'.[5]

Some benefactors prefer to remain anonymous and collaborate unobtrusively in a joint project, but others prefer to specify the exact destination of their funds and identify themselves. This has long been so, whether an afterlife seemed a reality or not. 'Wherever we look among the social elite of early modern England', Sir Keith Thomas writes, 'we find that fame was the spur, the acknowledged incentive to perform deeds of merit'.[6] In our own time, for several million pounds an entire building might be named, sometimes also with named areas within it. There is also the pleasure of putting your hand on the wall and saying 'this is our bit'. It is a pleasure that can be quite widely 'sold off': £1 million for a named lecture room, £500,000 for an entrance hall, £100,000 for a seminar room, and plaques on seats in lecture and dining halls can go for a few hundred, though lavatories do not seem to be on offer. Fundraisers distribute brochures with shopping-lists and prices attached. The initiative in naming can also, of course, come from the donor. When I was Wolfson's chief executive I quite often went to see a new facility which my charity had funded, and if the

---

[4] *The Times*, 25 Aug. 1990, pp. 11, 22.

[5] University of Oxford, *Annual Review, 2001/2002*, p. 22.

[6] K. V. Thomas, *The Ends of Life: Roads to Fulfilment in Early Modern England* (Oxford, 2009), p. 237.

topic had not arisen already I'd ask, before departing, 'now tell me, where is it that you are going to put the plaque?' The naming of charities after the donor isn't always straightforward: one surname may be fine, and even a first name and surname might be acceptable. But what about 'The Mary-Lou Smith and John Paul Jones Jun. Institute', not unknown, especially in the U.S.A?

My third question concerns how far benefactors should be free to attach conditions to their proposed grant, such as influencing a building's architecture and design. A university will usually have drawn up detailed plans for the building before fundraising begins, plans which reflect its own taste or its environment. On the other hand, major funders might well not want their names attached to buildings that they think are carbuncles. And the building, once funded, requires maintenance: a donor or foundation have their own name and image to preserve and might reasonably expect the building to be kept in good repair, inside and out. Chairmen, trustees or chief executives have been known to visit buildings that they have funded with a view to monitoring their interior decoration and maintenance, or indeed to inspect the washrooms. Such philanthropic 'interference' is not necessarily negative. After all, academics are not the only people with good ideas: the benefactor's influence may be beneficial, whether on conception or execution, on financial aspects or on subjects covered. I recall instances where questions inspired by the donor's business background cut costs; alternatively, the donor may decide to give more, so as to deal with the problem: for example, to improve the standard student rooms or make the building more attractive, or promote the study of a particular subject.

Some philanthropists (or possibly trustees acting as their agents) transfer to the charitable world the risk-taking that is widespread in business. The Nuffield Foundation pointed out in 1956 that private philanthropy

> finances projects that may yield dividends not in terms of cash but of public good. It is a risk-taking bank. It is least interested in secure investments which will produce a modest return. It is out for high dividends and can afford to balance its failures against its successes. Its first concern must be the credit-worthiness of the applicant; its second, the originality of his idea; its third, the soundness of his project.[7]

In taking forward their aims they may not confine beneficiaries to those who apply, but seek more highly qualified executors. Or, as the secretary of

---

[7] Quoted in L. E. Waddilove, *Private Philanthropy and Public Welfare: the Joseph Rowntree Memorial Trust 1954–1979* (1983), p. 17, quoting the Nuffield Foundation's 11th report (1955/6).

the Carnegie Trust put it more succinctly in 1952, 'it is the business of trusts to live dangerously'.[8]

Integral to discussing the philanthropist's 'interference' is the question of timescale. For how long can a charity reasonably expect a beneficiary to lodge a donation in its institutional memory? I have on occasion visited a university holding a list of the grants it has earlier received, and when I asked about a named laboratory for which a grant had been made twenty or thirty years before, nobody quite knew where it was or for what it was now used, perhaps because the nature of the research for which it was originally designated had lost significance. It could have been difficult for the university to commit itself in perpetuity to the donor, and yet the funds might never have been forthcoming without any such promise. A further problem is that names can sometimes quite quickly come to seem unsuitable, or go out of fashion. For example, Hearing Dogs recently organized an anniversary event (essentially a fundraising event, as these occasions usually now are) which the then prime minister attended. One might have thought that the presentation of 'Cameron', the puppy, to the prime minister was uncontentious enough at the time; yet as we all know, 'a week is a long time in politics'.

My fourth question highlights the potential tension which arises between the wishes of the founder and the machinery that implements them. 'I am essentially what may be called a strong man' said Dr. Barnardo, 'i.e. I rule'.[9] How many twentieth-century benefactors could say such a thing? It is now quite common for benefactors to set up a charity as the vehicle for their philanthropy. There are advantages such as tax relief, as well as establishing a means of allocating funds arising from an endowment when they are no longer personally involved. But organizations with charitable status must comply with increasingly stringent regulatory requirements.

Even since I joined the sector in 1997 there have been significant increases in state regulation of charities. Some such changes are well justified, especially on the need to scrutinize the proportion of the funds allocated to administration, to make it clear that they aim at the public benefit, and to publicize their policy on reserves, investment and managing risk. For fundraising charities, new rules are also now being introduced to prevent harassment through unwanted phone calls and the like.

And charities are run by boards of trustees. Such boards may consist of family members, friends and business associates, or experts appointed for their knowledge of the fields within which the charity operates. The

---

[8] D. Owen, *English Philanthropy, 1660–1960* (Oxford, 1965), p. 557.
[9] S. L. Barnardo and J. Marchant, *Memoirs of the late Dr. Barnardo* (1907), p. 300.

benefactor will probably chair the charity initially, but the trustee body as a whole has the responsibility for the proper running of the charity and indeed has the power to outvote the founder.

The founder's or the trustees' qualities or time commitment may well not extend to the day-to-day management of a charity. Hence the emergence within the charitable world of executive heads. As well as administering the allocation of funds, it is their job to ensure that the board of trustees has the information and assistance needed to comply with regulatory requirements. Who are these executives? Without systematic analysis I have noticed that during the past half-century there has been a shift in the charitable sector from senior ex-servicemen (and they *were* men) to senior or just-retired public-sector workers or business people, and later to those whose careers have advanced within the charitable world. These changes bring losses and gains. A life spent entirely in the charitable sector risks a lack of comparative perspective and breadth of experience, but it has the advantage of rendering the charity familiar with the growing and increasingly complex regulation in this area, as well as accumulated experience of working with the board of trustees which takes the decisions. And, yes, there are now more women chief executives.

How are the executives of funding bodies regarded by potential beneficiaries? Here the situations of the public and private sector differ. If the funder (acting for the taxpayer) is in the public sector, applicants may feel prejudice against what they regard as the irritating face of bureaucracy. A charity may in its relations with applicants benefit from inheriting some of the deference due to founders, and sometimes also from the relatively small size of the provider. In both situations, however, there is a certain friction when it comes to dealing with the application. The applicants must tolerate stipulations on length and format, given that competing claims have to be assessed and the assessors' burden curbed. Applicants to a charity may worry about whether the executives know enough about their field to select the right reviewers and can run an efficient peer-review process. I found that applicants were usually civil, especially as one became more senior, and they could never be sure how far the executive could influence the decision, which does indeed vary between charities. And dealing with us was a means to their end. In the Wolfson Foundation we always emphasized that we ran our own peer-review system, and that it was the trustees who reached decisions.

Nevertheless, I was often told that giving money away must be a lovely job. In many ways it was. There was great satisfaction when – after seeing proposals on paper, guiding an applicant through the application process, obtaining expert opinions, drawing the requisite information to trustees' attention, and obtaining a positive outcome – the day arrived when one could go along to see a new building or facilities in use. On the other hand, there were the disappointed applicants to be faced, and difficulty in knowing how far to accept offers of hospitality from the hopeful. If one's charity funded projects in the arts, how often was it reasonable (taking an extreme example) to accept an invitation to the opera? Confronted with a preliminary inquiry about funding, it was important to know what was being promoted, and sometimes this required having a look. After an award had been made, it might also be reasonable to see the completed project. But it usually seemed sensible not to accept invitations while an application was under consideration, and to conduct discussions about an application in the office rather than over lunch. But yes, it is true that overall – even though not all applications succeed – a certain popularity as chief executive is pleasant. My husband wryly observed on one social occasion that I had been kissed by seventeen vice-chancellors – though one knows all too well that from retirement day their flow of Christmas cards shrinks and their kisses cease.

7. Calibrating relevance at the Pitt Rivers Museum

Laura N. K. Van Broekhoven

Public institutions such as schools, hospitals, universities and museums hope that they can be of direct personal relevance to stakeholders and wider constituencies. The concept of relevance is studied in many fields including cognitive sciences, logic and epistemology. In institutional terms, it involves being meaningful to society at large, and in practical terms, for a museum at least, it will involve satisfying the needs of broader audiences. Given that relevance is, in its nature, temporary, and is spatially, institutionally and individually bound, institutions need to constantly adjust themselves to remain relevant. Relevance is ascribed and needs to be intentionally cultivated. It is not something, therefore, that an institution can assign to itself nor is it static: institutions need to constantly adjust themselves to remain relevant. How does a museum ensure that users find inspiration, enchantment and knowledge that are of direct personal relevance?

Relevance

In a recent book on *The Art of Relevance*, Nina Simon debunks two of the commonly held myths around relevance and museums.[1] First, the idea of universal relevance: the belief among museum professionals that what we do is relevant to everyone, always. Compare this with the concept of relative relevance which suggests that information is relevant to people at certain times and will depend on their own interests and/or life experiences. Second, that 'relevance is irrelevant': an often firm belief that visitors will be so mesmerized by the awesomeness and distinctiveness of what museums do that they do not need to be convinced of our relevance. This attitude may inhibit us from actively reaching out and finding ways to connect to new audiences, ways which would lead to change and increased relevance; it might prevent us from creating and opening doors to audiences to which we would like to be relevant. Simon's definition of relevance is inspired by cognitive scientists Deirdre Wilson and Dan Sperber who believe that

[1] N. Simon, *The Art of Relevance* (Santa Cruz, Calif., 2016).

L. N. K. Van Broekhoven, 'Calibrating relevance at the Pitt Rivers Museum', in *Dethroning historical reputations: universities, museums and the commemoration of benefactors*, ed. J. Pellew and L. Goldman (2018), pp. 65–79.

relevance needs to involve something that yields positive cognitive effects:[2] 'Something is relevant if it gives you new information, if it adds meaning to your life, if it makes a difference to you … that … brings new value to the table'. A museum, Simon argues, matters when it matters to people.[3]

An entire set of measuring sticks is used on and by museums such as the Pitt Rivers Museum (P.R.M.) to measure success, impact and relevance: visitor numbers (physical and virtual), awards and recognitions, publications, number of outgoing loans etc. Our Museum, usually, scores rather well on most accounts. While museums on the Continent and elsewhere in Britain are battling falling numbers of visitors, and are spending hundreds of thousands of pounds or euros to make special exhibitions more attractive, the visitor numbers of the P.R.M. have been rising for over a decade. Today the museum is open every day of the week, and receives nearly 450,000 visitors per year.[4]

Unlike other museums of its kind, in the P.R.M. objects are exhibited according to type, rather than geographical region, or time period. Today, its typological arrangement functions as a 'democracy of things', revealing fascinating distinctions between and across cultures. This encourages reflection, which can be compelling and challenging in equal measure. However, its layout is rooted in Victorian-era ideas of social evolution, and even though the collections have multiple biographies, a significant quantity of them were amassed under British colonial aspiration, rule and expansion. The Museum is much-loved for its characteristic multi-layered and dense displays, but has also been scrutinized, particularly in postcolonial writing, for unquestioningly repeating colonial paradigms (or so it seems) by embedding these in the very fabric of its collections and displays.

Does its immense popularity, evident in its visitor numbers, prove that the P.R.M. matters? And if so, what are the implications of that? How do we ensure that the typological displays are relevant today, not as a testament to human/social evolution, but as a celebration of our common humanity and as a means to bridge differences? Can it help encourage global cross-cultural reflection and cultural competence? Or is it doomed to remain a 'preserve of colonialism'?[5]

---

2 D. Wilson and D. Sperber, *Meaning and Relevance* (Cambridge, 2012), p. 62.

3 Simon, *The Art of Relevance*, p. 29.

4 Most Continental ethnographic museums receive between 120,000 and 200,000 visitors per year with far larger marketing budgets.

5 C. Kravagna, 'The preserve of colonialism: the world in the museum', *European Institute for Progressive Culture Policies*, 2008 (transl. Tim Sharp) <http://eipcp.net/transversal/0708/kravagna/en> [accessed 16 Apr. 2018].

To calibrate

In order to consider how a museum that is so quintessentially nineteenth-century in character can be relevant in the contemporary world I propose using the concept of 'calibration'. This term describes how we constantly re-adjust ourselves to remain relevant to our audiences and how those adjustments are intended both to open doors to new audiences and often lead to more accurate narratives. These adjustments are necessary to ensure the sustainable relevance of the institution.

The *Oxford Encyclopaedia* defines the verb 'to calibrate' as:

1. To correlate the readings of (an instrument) with those of a standard in order to check the instrument's accuracy.

2. To adjust (experimental results) to take external factors into account or to allow comparison with other data.

3. To carefully assess, set, or adjust (something abstract).[6]

For people who work with machinery or instruments concerned with measurement it seems all too obvious that over time there is a tendency for results and accuracy to 'drift' from the standard, especially when using specific technologies or measuring particular parameters. Also, one accepts that standards vary from country to country, depending upon the type of industry or applications and that to ensure reliable, accurate and repeatable measurements there is an ongoing need to service and maintain the calibration of equipment throughout its lifetime. Now, museums are surely not merely measuring instruments, but one might argue that they do need regular servicing or calibrating. Museums have had a varied role throughout history and they have often had to readjust, or undergo a process of 'carefully assessing, setting or adjusting' that takes external factors into account.

Calibration also involves, for example in archaeology when assessing Carbon-14 readings, adjustment to account for long-term and shorter-term variations, and the use of probabilistic methods to calculate an acceptable range to interpret the readings and transfer them to a calendar date. Recently, again in archaeology, important shifts were unanimously adopted by practitioners to formerly accepted readings. Through a method of Bayesian inference methodologies, the output probability distributions were improved and new interpretations on long-accepted dates were proposed and accepted unanimously. As more historical data became available, and new techniques of analysis were applied, readings were readily adapted by the field.[7] Could the same be done for museums? How would a

---

[6] <https://en.oxforddictionaries.com/definition/calibrate> [accessed 16 Apr. 2018].
[7] R. C. Bronk, 'Bayesian analysis of radiocarbon dates', *Radiocarbon*, li (2009), 337–60.

Victorian-age museum calibrate itself to ensure relevance in the twenty-first century? There are three key questions here: what external factors should be considered, what is the 'standard', and given these, how might we adjust?

'*To correlate with a standard to check accuracy*'

The Pitt Rivers Museum was founded in 1884 and was opened to the public between 1887 and 1892.[8] The museum is located at the back of the Oxford University Museum of Natural History on South Parks Road and forms part of the University of Oxford. For a long time it was open for only two hours a day and would receive small numbers of visitors at a time.

The museum was founded through a generous gift of over 27,000 objects donated by General Augustus Lane Fox, a well-known nineteenth-century collector of archaeological and ethnographic objects.[9] The general moved in academic circles that included many of the most prominent British intellectuals of his time. Though a military man, it was through his 1853 marriage with Alice Stanley that he was welcomed into her family's more intellectual circle of friends. The thinking of some of the most important minds of the Victorian age, including biologist Charles Darwin, archaeologist Flinders Petrie and philosopher Herbert Spencer, heavily influenced the general's collecting practices. The latter's theories on sociocultural evolutionism (and moralism) were central to the general's thinking on material culture.[10] His earliest collections and displays (of firearms, weaponry from around the world, boomerangs and lock-key sets) were arranged chronologically to illustrate how they developed over time from the more rudimentary to the more complex.[11]

General Pitt Rivers was driven by a strong desire for public education and was particularly interested in museums as places where minds could be

---

[8] A. Petch, 'Notes on the opening of the Pitt Rivers Museum', *Jour. Museum Ethnography,* xix (March 2007), 101–12.

[9] Later in his life the general adopted the name Pitt Rivers when his cousin, Horace Pitt, the 6th Baron Rivers, died without heirs and left the Rivers estate to the general on the condition that he prove willing to adopt the surname Pitt Rivers and the Pitt family coat of arms (see M. Bowden, *Pitt Rivers: the Life and Archaeological Work of Lieutenant-General Augustus Henry Lane Fox Pitt Rivers, DCL, FRS, FSA* (Cambridge, 1991)). The general abruptly became the owner of 27,000 acres, making him one of the largest landowners in the country.

[10] Darwin himself was never convinced that social evolution was analogous to biological evolution (see J. Howard, *Darwin,* v (Oxford, 1982), quoted in Bowden, *Pitt Rivers,* at p. 48).

[11] M. O'Hanlon, *The Pitt Rivers Museum: a World Within* (London and Oxford, 2014), pp. 24–5, 28–9.

shaped. He was acutely aware of the fact that museums, if they were to be places of public education, needed to open their doors to wider audiences. To do that they needed to find doors that were of relevance to those audiences and therefore: 'must be supplemented by other inducements to make them attractive'.[12] In his museum in Farnham (a second museum he built after having donated his collections to the University of Oxford) there were picnic bowers, dining halls, statues, a temple, an open-air theatre, a band-stand, a race-course and a golf course. It was by finding what mattered to them that Pitt Rivers made the museum in Farnham relevant. Visitor figures to the estate were very high: in 1899, for example, 44,417 visitors were recorded. At the end of the nineteenth century, the general was convinced that museums could be used as spaces in which to persuade lay audiences that the answers to the future were in evolution not revolution.[13]

In Oxford, the museum that was named after the general and the one I currently direct was driven by a similar quest for public education. A panel placed near the museum's entrance in the 1890s explained the 'arrangement and object of this collection'.[14] None of the original 'objectives' of the museum – showing how objects evolve from the simpler to the complex; explaining the conservatism of 'savage races'; demonstrating 'how progress has been effected'; illustrating the corresponding stages of civilization that 'savages' go through etc. – correspond at all with the museum's current mission statement, nor with the vision outlined in our Strategic Plan for 2017–22: 'to build and share knowledge about humanity's many ways of knowing, being, creating and coping in our interconnected worlds with the widest possible audience'. We see our displays as a celebration of human creativity that encourage global cross-cultural reflection, and as a tribute to cultural diversity. In a world that is increasingly divided, can we mobilize our collections, our displays and our space to bring people closer together, to engage with each other more respectfully, out of curiosity not prejudice, looking beyond binaries and searching for possibilities?

One of our guiding principles is to aim to be 'part of a process of redress and social healing and the mending of historically difficult relationships'.

---

[12] A. H. L. F. Pitt Rivers, 'Typological museums, as exemplified by the Pitt Rivers Museum at Oxford, and his provincial museum at Farnham, Dorset', *Jour. Society of Arts,* xl (1891), 115–22.

[13] 'The knowledge of the facts of evolution, and of the processes of gradual development, is the one great knowledge that we have to inculcate' (Pitt Rivers, 'Typological museums' (1891)) <http://web.prm.ox.ac.uk/rpr/index.php/article-index/12-articles/189-typological-museums.html> [accessed 16 Apr. 2018].

[14] Information Panel, PRM Papers, Box 11, Item 7 in O'Hanlon, *The Pitt Rivers Museum,* p. 54.

And we aim to be a listening and learning organization that inspires creativity in all its many forms. But are we?

'To adjust to take external factors into account'

The P.R.M. is proud to be appreciated by its audiences. So much so that both in more formal benchmarking exercises (the Association of Leading Visitor Attractions – A.L.V.A.) and via online customer feedback channels on social media (Facebook, Yelp, Google, TripAdvisor), we score among the highest in the U.K. As with many other visitor attractions in the U.K., the P.R.M. is benchmarked by the A.L.V.A. Visitors indicate they want to broaden their horizons and see the museum as a trusted source of information worth visiting. Of all U.K. A.L.V.A. visitor destinations, the P.R.M. receives the highest 'Net Promoter Score' that measures the overall likelihood of whether one would promote a visit to others (+87 for P.R.M., average +60). Also, of all participating A.L.V.A. members the P.R.M. receives the highest score in terms of 'value for money' (9.4 for P.R.M., average 8.3).

Over 600,000 ethnographic and archaeological objects, photographs, films, sound recordings and manuscripts from every area of the world are kept in the Museum's collections, each with its own biography, and pedigree. 55,000 of those are on display and nearly all are shared with global audiences through online databases. The extraordinary range of objects that form the collections of the Museum have been assembled from all over the world and are testament to social networks forged over time and in very different sorts of conditions, some being the result of colonial exploitation and duress, others the result of long-lasting deep friendships, academic research or diplomatic ties.[15]

A quick review of visitors' comments – online, in visitor books at the entrance, in published tour guides and in newspaper articles in the national and international press – does not show much critical reflection on how the collection or displays are interwoven with the legacies of empire. Apart from praise like: 'friendly staff', 'the best museum in the world', 'could spend hours', 'great for all ages', 'amazing collection' and 'free entry', frequently mentioned tropes include 'shrunken heads', 'totem poles', 'treasure trove', 'Indiana Jones', 'Grandmother's Attic' and 'Aladdin's cave'. Thus, in reviewing the Museum, people tend to call on iconic images from popular culture that might seem innocent at first glance, but considered more carefully also bring to mind unsettling racialized stereotypes that could be considered to have their roots in Orientalism,

[15] For example, see <http://web.prm.ox.ac.uk/england/englishness-english-databases.html> [accessed 16 Apr. 2018].

colonialism or racism. To refer to a place as an Aladdin's cave is to say that place contains many interesting or valuable objects. The cave, inspired by Ali Baba's cave from 'Arabian Nights', refers to an amazing place, where all manner of goods are stored, conveying an idea of mystery, awe and (hidden) wealth (that is, 'Les contes des mille et une nuits' in French). The reference to Aladdin immediately brings to mind the racialized stereotypical representation of Arab individuals in the 1992 Disney film.[16] Similarly, to describe something as a 'treasure trove' means that it is a very good or rich source of something. In the U.K., the expression also had a legal implication up until 1996, suggesting it was connected to a law where valuable articles, such as coins, bullion, etc. found hidden in the earth or elsewhere, and of unknown ownership, would become the property of the crown (which compensated the finder if the treasure was declared). In 1996 'treasure' was legally defined as any item over 300 years old and containing more than 5 per cent precious metal. The reference to Indiana Jones, similarly conjures up images of tomb looting, and of 'rescuing' objects from failing nation states or peoples who cannot take care of their own heritage.

The Shrunken Heads (or *tsantsas*) of the Pitt Rivers Museum are generally seen as 'one of the best-known displays of human remains of Latin American origin in the UK' and are specifically mentioned by numerous newspaper articles and tourist reviews.[17] They are often seen as one of the hallmarks of the museum and, anecdotally, the museum's front of house staff report the three questions most commonly asked by visitors coming through the door are: 'where are the toilets?', 'where is the café?' and 'where are the Shrunken Heads?'. Interviews with visitors looking at the display carried out in 2003, reveal that many people think of these objects as 'primitive', referring to them as 'gory, gruesome, barbaric, mystical, a freak show, unnatural'. People reported feeling 'strangeness' and feeling 'disgusted' and felt that the exhibit sparked their interest out of 'morbid curiosity' and brought up 'primal feelings'.[18] These responses suggest that

[16] 'The film's light-skinned lead characters, Aladdin and Jasmine, have Anglicized features and Anglo-American accents. This is in contrast to the other characters who are dark-skinned, swarthy and villainous – cruel palace guards or greedy merchants with Arabic accents and grotesque facial features ... the film immediately characterizes the Arab world as alien, exotic, and "other." Arab Americans see this film as perpetuating the tired stereotype of the Arab world as a place of deserts and camels, of arbitrary cruelty and barbarism.' (The American Arab Anti-Discrimination Committee <http://www.adc.org/2009/11/arab-stereotypes-and-american-educators/> [accessed 16 Apr. 2018]).

[17] P. Gordon, '"Tongued with fire": encounters with museum visitors and displayed human remains' (unpublished University of London Ph.D. thesis, 2009), p. 18.

[18] P. Gordon, 'Life after death: the social transformation of Tsantsas', in 'Material

instead of helping visitors better understand the practice of headhunting, many saw the exhibit as a metaphor for the primitive behaviour of 'others'. On the other hand, other interviewees felt the same exhibits encouraged people to acknowledge cultural diversity and to develop a broader 'world view', as well as 'sparking curiosity' to learn more about other people's cultures.[19] In other museums Shuar and Ashuar representatives (present-day descendants of the makers of the *tsantsas*) have argued either for the return, contextualization or removal from display of *tsantsas* as they no longer wish their culture only to be 'represented' through these 'powerful visual anchors for stereotyping'.[20] Rubenstein has argued, convincingly, that the displaying of shrunken heads, more than many other objects in museums: 'provoke ambivalent feelings about the past and uncertainties about their meanings in the present'. For museum curators and visitors, he says, 'they indicate the power of a museum to represent the whole world under one roof, but they also represent a distasteful obsession with savagery left over from the age of colonial expansion and exploration'. There is no simple answer to whether or not the *tsantsas* should or should not remain on display as they are and can be read in many ways. 'For Shuar, they recall the power and independence of their fathers or grandfathers, but they also remind them of a time when escalating warfare devastated many Shuar households, in some cases reducing their population by half'.[21] At the same time they are also seen to be functioning as ambassadors of Shuar culture: 'the presence of the heads in the museum expressed North American interest in Shuar culture', representing thereby 'a Shuar presence in the centre of the world'.[22]

In particular, indigenous scholars and activists have criticized ethnographic museums for interpreting cultures through practices of 'othering'. Locking objects, and the people that made them, in static representations can have the effect of objectifying and manipulating them so that they can fit categories and outlooks that are alien to the individuals who forged and designed the objects. This often involves eliminating the sacral or cultural dimensions of the objects in order that they can be

---

anthropology and museum ethnography of the Institute of Social and Cultural Anthropology' (unpublished University of Oxford M.Sc. thesis, 2003), p. 32.

[19] Gordon, 'Life after death', p. 36.

[20] S. L. Rubenstein, 'Shuar migrants and shrunken heads face to face in a New York museum', *Anthropology Today*, xx (2004), 15–18. See also R. W. West, *All Roads are Good: Native Voices on Life and Culture* (Washington, D.C., 1994); L. Peers, *Shrunken Heads* (Oxford, 2011).

[21] S. L. Rubenstein, 'Crossing boundaries and shrunken heads', in *Border Crossings: Transnational Americanist Anthropology*, ed. K. S. Fine-Dare and S. L. Rubenstein (Lincoln, Nebr., 2009), p. 128.

[22] S. L. Rubenstein, 'Crossing boundaries' (2009), p. 142.

understood by onlookers.[23] Simply taking the *tsantsas* off display without entering into conversations with Shuar and Ashuar descendants on how they would prefer to be represented within the museum would be a missed opportunity for inviting in voices that need to be heard by audiences who we know are interested in broadening their horizons.

In recent years, the museum has undergone much critical introspection, published extensively on practices of collecting, made changes in our public programmes, and undertaken extensive work with indigenous peoples on reconnecting historical collections with present-day stakeholders. Visitors' comments indicate that despite this work we have still not found a compelling way of translating that thinking and teaching into the permanent displays and galleries, so that instead of finding confirmation of stereotypical images and concepts, visitors coming into the museum develop a deeper understanding of humanity's many ways of knowing, being and coping through time.

'To carefully assess, set or adjust'

On 23 October 2015, *Rhodes Must Fall* tweeted that the 'Pitt-Rivers museum is one of the most violent spaces in Oxford'. Brian Kwoba, at the time a Rhodes Scholar and doctoral student at Oxford, wrote an article in *Cherwell*, the student newspaper, explaining that the university:

> is choked with various Rhodes-like products of colonial plunder, from the Codrington Library at All Souls College, which was endowed with money from Christopher Codrington's colonial slave plantations in Barbados, to the Pitt Rivers Museum which houses thousands of artefacts stolen from colonised peoples throughout the world.[24]

Similar calls to decolonize disciplines, institutions and methodologies have been made insistently both in academic literature and elsewhere.[25] A wide range of protests erupted in 2015 and 2016 across the U.S., continental Europe and the U.K., which questioned colonial paradigms, orientalism, gentrification and the impact they have on museums. The following are a few specific examples. The 2012 to 2016 #DecolonizeTheMuseum Critical

[23] L. N. K. Van Broekhoven, 'Ethnographic heterotopia' ('Proceedings of the International Colloquium: do Ethnographic Museums Need Ethnography?' Rome: Pigorini Museum, 17–19 Apr. 2012).

[24] B. Kwoba, see <http://www.cherwell.org/2015/06/12/rhodes-must-fall-here-and-now> [accessed 30 July 2017].

[25] A. Lonetree, *Decolonizing Museums: Representing Native America in National and Tribal Museums* (Chapel Hill, N.C., 2012); see also L. T. Smith, *Decolonizing Methodologies: Research and Indigenous Peoples* (London and New York, 1999 and 2012).

Communities' Collective in the Netherlands named its cause as being to decolonize Dutch ethnographic museums. A 'Decolonize this place' protest was staged outside the American Museum of Natural History in New York City on 10 October 2016; several protests took place at the Museum of Fine Arts in Boston under the banner 'Decolonize our Museums' (D.O.M.), and the Decolonial Cultural Front (D.C.F.) held protests in 2016 at the Brooklyn Museum.[26]

As elsewhere, at Oxford persistent challenges are being made – particularly by grassroots and student movements such as 'Rhodes Must Fall' and 'Common Ground' – that highlight enduring structures and symbols of inequality and oppression and call for these to be altered. Clearly, the P.R.M. does not escape such criticism, and, as its director, I know that even though for many of our visitors the museum belongs in the category of one their 'all-time favourite museums in the world' (often nostalgically transporting people back to the magical years of their youth), the museum can be interpreted differently by our audiences, depending on personal biography and visual literacy. More than most other museums, the P.R.M. is seen as a museum whose very space contains echoes of empire. With its 'museum of the museum' aura it seemingly breathes life into a celebration of colonialism instead of contesting it or engaging with it.

In a place like the P.R.M. time seems to be frozen, and visitors and volunteers alike indicate they feel one of the most difficult elements to grasp in the museum is the concept of time: how do things relate to each other? Yet, as one would expect of a museum of international repute, when one looks more closely at interpretation labels, teaching, displays, current acquisitions and publications, it becomes apparent that most of the original 1890s 'arrangement' of the displays and collection strategies no longer apply to current practices. According to some, the museum has already 'radically changed its discourse'.[27] And, to a large degree, it has.

---

[26] These protests also challenge the gentrification and displacement unfolding just outside the marble walls of museums, in poor communities of colour of the surrounding city that are excluded from what are considered more elite cultural spheres; they are typically action-oriented and some are becoming more and more intersectional, putting indigenous struggle, black liberation, free Palestine, global wage workers and de-gentrification at their centre (<http://conversations.e-flux.com/t/what-does-it-mean-to-decolonize-a-museum/5084> [accessed 17 Apr. 2018]; <http://www.decolonizethisplace.org> [accessed 17 Apr. 2018]).

[27] A. Sauvage, 'To be or not to be colonial: museums facing their exhibitions', *Culturales*, vi (2010), 110.

This is less easily visible to our visitors, however, than we might ideally want it to be now and in the future. In 1998, with a new director and two new lecturer-curators in post, the staff held a discussion on the question 'What should an ethnographic museum be in the twenty-first century?' According to one staff member present, 'the subtext was, should we rip it all out and start again'. It was agreed that the historic nature of the displays had value as an articulation of Britain's encounters with other peoples, and given other pressing issues facing the museum at that time (the need to re-roof and add insulation, the need for major funding and research grants) the consensus was 'not to tinker with the displays too much and to focus on scholarly and collaborative research behind the scenes, publishing online for the public and in academic venues'.[28] This decision to 'respect the special visual spirit of the displays' and concentrate on the development of new practices around the collections was, therefore, a deliberate strategy chosen at a particular moment in time which made sense given other simultaneous institutional needs. It led to numerous pioneering and invaluable projects around the documentation of the collection, the production of award-winning online resources and much innovative collaborative museum work with originating communities. It also stimulated the development of an unrivalled open research policy through fully accessible online databases that not only provide all our available data in an easily searchable format, but include comments made during visits by scholars and the wider cultural sector – by global standards this is an exceptional feature for a museum. Online resources have been transformative for their respective fields such as *The Tibet Album* website project, used widely by Tibetan scholars and Tibetans living in exile; *The Kainai Visual Repatriation Project* that inspired colleagues across the globe to initiate similar projects; *Scoping Museum Anthropology* (http://web.prm.ox.ac.uk/sma/) that made unique primary historic documents available online; and many more.

Nonetheless, in contrast to European museums, which have attempted to refashion themselves by renaming and refurbishment as part of a process of 'rebirthing' (for example, the Musée du Quai Branly in Paris or the VärldskulturMuseum in Gotenburg), the P.R.M. has been held up as an example of a museum that attests to the 'denial of coevalness'. This is in reference to Fabian's seminal analysis in *Time and the Other* of the persistent and systematic tendency to place the object of anthropology in a time other than the present of the producer or subject of anthropological discourse. This 'present tense', declares Fabian, 'freezes a society at the time

---

[28] P.R.M. staff member, Laura Peers, personal communication.

of observation; at worst, it contains assumptions about the repetitiveness, predictability and conservativism of primitives'.[29]

Changing lightbulbs[30]

Linda Alcoff maintains that in 'certain privileged locations' it can be 'discursively dangerous' to speak for others.[31] In other words, when the privileged speak for or on behalf of the less privileged, it has the result of increasing or reinforcing the oppression of the group spoken for. The Pitt Rivers Museum certainly seems to qualify as one of these 'privileged locations': set in the University of Oxford and filled with objects from across the world. Museums and their staff, especially university museums, like the P.R.M., are seen to be authorities on their collections and their display, and often that involves processes of both inclusion and exclusion of voices.

In recent decades, different ethnographic museums have acknowledged that indigenous peoples, racialized minorities, and stakeholder communities are authorities on their own cultures and have set up more collaborative ways of working. This has demonstrated that where joint expertise is shared – and authority is negotiated (rather than assumed) – new light shines on collections, and new contemporary relevance is revealed that enables museums to become part of the processes of healing and redress. Such collaborations involve the willingness to work towards co-creative knowledge production and to see museum objects not merely as 'things' but as potentially animate, as embodying sets of relationships, as having personhood and needing cultural care as much as physical preservation or interpretation.

Members of the P.R.M.'s academic, collections, education and conservation staff have been at the forefront of developing and trialling this sort of collaborative work and have published extensively on it to critical acclaim. Owing to strategic choices made in the past, that critical writing and thinking has been concentrated on work 'behind the scenes' that can be found online and in our publications, but it is now ready to be translated to our more permanent displays. In other words, the 'static' public face of our museum does not always reflect that we are at the forefront of

---

[29] J. Fabian, *Time and the Other: How Anthropology makes its Objects* (New York, N.Y., 1983), p. 80. See also Kravanga.

[30] This subtitle refers to a 'joke' I was told over and over when I arrived at Oxford to take up my post as director. At least a dozen people independently told me the same joke each time I mentioned the word change: 'How many Oxford professors does it take to change a lightbulb?' … the answer: '*change?*'.

[31] L. Alcoff, 'The problem of speaking for others', *Cultural Critique*, xx (1991–2), 5–32.

establishing collaborative museology, opening doors to previously uninvited communities, engaging with stakeholders near and far. In consequence, we are ready to ask the next questions and are engaging in qualitative audience research into the experience of non-specialist visitors when they walk through the galleries. What messages do they find? What sides of the stories do we tell, and which ones do we not touch upon? Which parts do we silence, and which do we voice?

We might seem to have inherited the most difficult space in which to try to achieve this. But it could be argued that an intrinsically imperial and Victorian museum such as the P.R.M. makes us the perfect space in which to engage with, and address such issues and responses. We must also set out ideas for making new acquisitions that ensure that our collections connect with the contemporary as much as they reflect the past. Until now, interpretation at the P.R.M. (object labels, audio guides and display texts) has striven to be 'as neutral as possible'. As I have argued elsewhere, this 'neutrality' does not exist. We are always careful to use certain words and avoid others. If we interrogate the language we use, the visual representations in our displays, on our web and in our special exhibitions or promotional material, it becomes clear that some of the language we have uncritically adopted actually perpetuates the very representational issues and stereotypical misconceptions outlined above, rather than enabling our visitors to question them, and move beyond them.

I want to ensure that in the future when we talk about, for example, the Cook voyages, we consciously use historically accurate descriptions and avoid perpetuating ideas of Pacific Romanticism born from a European imagination. On labels, do we continue to talk about the Britons' 'arrival,' calling them 'traders', 'missionaries' and 'colonial powers', instead of using other, more recently proposed terminology, that is seen as more historically accurate and cannot be interpreted as euphemistic?[32] In the future, when we re-display or work with the Benin Bronzes, how do we more poignantly address the violent nature of the punitive campaigns that brought the collections here as loot and then sold the objects to museums in Europe to cover the cost of those same campaigns? We are setting up collaborations with a diversity of partners across the globe and also in Oxford to engage critically with these questions and provide alternatives to the institutional voice and the accepted narratives.

---

[32] University of New South Wales, Sydney, *Indigenous Terminology*, 2016 <https://teaching.unsw.edu.au/indigenous-terminology> [accessed 17 Apr. 2018].

Concluding remarks

Museums tend to fulfil many functions at once: a meeting place, a place for inspiration and reflection, a learning environment, a connector of communities and – more mundanely – a shelter from the rain. We know our displays and exhibitions can talk about humanity's many ways of knowing and many ways of being, of coping and creating, but we also know that it is only when we curate carefully and programme thoughtfully and with purpose that the displays will tell meaningful stories that will resonate with *all* our audiences and with the bigger issues facing the world today.

Much has been written about the benefits and limitations to the P.R.M. of its nineteenth-century layout and displays. For some, it remains a symbol of the Victorian colonialism that facilitated the building of those collections. But its very origin can also provoke a constructive response: because its 'displays are now so outdated ... they challenge visitors to consider what the European practice of collecting has meant to colonized peoples'.[33] And precisely because of its controversial inheritances, the P.R.M. has confronted and commented on its collections' colonial pasts more than many other museums. Nevertheless, that concepts and tropes such as 'treasure trove', 'Victorian grandeur' and 'colonial exploration' are named by a large quantity of the visitors in their comments – and largely as *positive* attributes – indicates that there is still some critical reflection and refurbishing that needs to be done as it relates to the construction of meaning and (un)conscious messaging.

Now, when we are being called 'one of the most Violent Spaces in Oxford' by student and grassroots movements, we must engage with criticism proactively and find ways to ensure that we change, though not by adapting a defensive position in which we try to show how much we have already achieved (and there is quite a bit), but by prioritizing what we have not yet done. We must also acknowledge that although processes of political decolonization might be more than seventy years old, the legacies of colonialism and empire continue to taint our understanding of the world and continue to influence its social contexts, political realities and historical records.[34]

We see our museum as intimately involved in the development of strategies that open up original pathways that help us cope with these tangled histories as part of a process of healing. We also see it as our duty, when necessary, to

[33] Sauvage, 'To be or not to be colonial', p. 110.

[34] W. D. Mignolo, *The Darker Side of Western Modernity* (Durham, N.C., 2011); *Echoes of Empire: Memory, Identity and the Legacy of Imperialism*, ed. K. Nicolaidis, B. Sèbe and G. Maas (2015).

acknowledge historical wrongs that lie at the root of the current politics of inequality, so that we can actively counter any perpetuation of colonialism and its consequent stereotyping and imbalances of power.

Taking into account the museum's current mission as outlined earlier, we are actively investing in becoming a museum that opens its doors to ensure that the audiences to which we hope to be of personal relevance both find us and feel at home in the museum. Looking at 'relevance' for the Pitt Rivers Museums involves engaging with difficult societal debates and political realities of today, so that in our galleries we can address the tension between repeating dominant histories and presenting alternative voices, telling histories of resistance without losing the opportunity to continue to amaze, inspire and spark curiosity for each other's creativity.

8. From objects of enlightenment to objects of apology: why you can't make amends for the past by plundering the present

Tiffany Jenkins

In early 2016, a brass cockerel that had stood in a student dining hall in Jesus College, Cambridge, became the focus of a lively repatriation claim. The Okukor, as it is known, is one of almost 1,000 Benin bronzes taken from Benin City, present-day Nigeria, during a punitive expedition by the British army in 1897. It had perched among the young scholars as they ate their meals in the college since 1930, when it was bequeathed by George William Neville, a member of the Benin Expedition, whose son had attended the college.

But not for much longer, student campaigners hoped. At a meeting of the Jesus College Student Union in March 2016, the Benin Bronze Appreciation Committee passed a motion which supported the repatriation of the Okukor to Nigeria. In a dense eleven-page document, the campaigners argued for 'returning [the artefact] to its place of origin'. Sending it back to the 'community from which it was stolen', they said, was 'just' – they wanted to return the cockerel to make amends for the 'sins' of British imperialism, continuing: 'the contemporary political culture surrounding colonialism and social justice, combined with the University's global agenda, offers a perfect opportunity for the College to benefit from this gesture'.[1] Following internal discussions, Cambridge University agreed that the statue should be taken down from its perch in the hall and the possibility of return considered. A University spokesperson said: 'Jesus College acknowledges the contribution made by the students in raising the important but complex question of the rightful location of its Benin bronze, in response to which it has permanently removed the Okukor from its hall'. It pledged to work with university authorities and museum professionals to 'discuss and determine the best future for the Okukor, including the question of repatriation'.[2]

[1] 'Jesus votes in cockerel row', *Varsity*, 18 Feb. 2016 <https://www.varsity.co.uk/news/9877> [accessed 17 Apr. 2018].

[2] 'Benin Bronze "permanently removed" from Jesus Hall', *The Cambridge Student*, 9 March 2016.

T. Jenkins, 'From objects of enlightenment to objects of apology: why you can't make amends for the past by plundering the present', in *Dethroning historical reputations: universities, museums and the commemoration of benefactors*, ed. J. Pellew and L. Goldman (2018), pp. 81–92.

On her blog, the racial equalities officer at Jesus College cheered this decision: 'It's nice to see Jesus [College] setting a precedent and taking steps in the right direction to weed out the colonial legacies that exist in bits of the university. We still have a lot of work to do ... but how exciting and momentous and revolutionary is this?!'[3] Joanna Williams, a lecturer in higher education at the University of Kent, took a different view, judging it a 'cowardly' move on behalf of the University and that 'students have declared war on the past and this is another example of how students are using history as a morality play to express their own moral superiority in the present'.[4]

Beyond the case of the cockerel, the repatriation of an object to its original location or people will, it is said, make amends for colonization, for the impact of settler societies, and for the harm that was done to conquered peoples hundreds of years ago. 'Cultural property turns out to be a particularly appropriate medium for negotiating historical injustices',[5] posits the historian Elazar Barkan. But is it? Why now are museum objects expected to repair the past? And what are the limitations to repatriation as a solution for historical injustice?

The origins of repatriation as an apology for past wrongs

The term 'reparations' was initially used in connection with fines exacted among states. It now refers to a broader project of making amends towards communities and individuals, as part of what the sociologists Jeffrey Olick and Brenda Coughlin characterize as the 'the politics of regret'. Olick and Coughlin describe the rise of a variety of movements for redress that have won some form of financial or symbolic compensation, including the restitution of objects and art as well as criminal prosecutions and public apologies, all of which have become prominent since the late 1980s. That is when the practice of making reparations went beyond those paid by the Germans to their Jewish victims from the Second World War and was extended to other groups for different historical wrongs. In a study on the vogue for historical contrition, the historian and geographer, David Lowenthal, identifies 1988 as the important turning point, when

[3] 'Cambridge college's bronze cockerel must go back to Nigeria, students say', *The Guardian*, 21 Feb. 2016

[4] 'Cambridge University agrees to remove Benin Bronze cockerel from the dining hall at Jesus College after students complained about its links to Britain's colonial past', *Daily Mail*, 8 March 2016

[5] E. Barkan, 'Restitution and amending historical injustices in international morality', in *Politics and the Past: on Repairing Historical Injustices*, ed. J. Torpey (Lanham, Md., 2003), p. 100.

the American government distributed $1.6 billion to Japanese-Americans who had been interned in camps during the war, by way of compensation. Lowenthal documents several subsequent reparations campaigns, with claimants from South Africa, Namibia, Argentina, Brazil and Chile, as well as Australian Aborigines, Native Americans, Japanese-Americans, and African-Americans.[6]

The historian Elazar Barkan locates the emergence of a new international moral order, based on apology for past acts, as emerging around the late 1990s. Barkan demonstrates that it was at this point that restitution for past victims became a major part of national politics and international diplomacy. He describes as a manifestation of this 'performative guilt' situations in which leaders theatrically say sorry for acts that they had no responsibility for from the past.[7] Examples more recently closer to the U.K. include when, one month after the British Conservative M.P. David Cameron became prime minister of a coalition government, in June 2010, he told the house of commons: 'I am deeply sorry' for an event that took place when he was five years old, that is the Bloody Sunday massacre of 1972, when British paratroopers opened fire on crowds at a civil rights demonstration in Derry/Londonderry in Northern Ireland. Two years later, Mr. Cameron was 'profoundly sorry' for the Hillsborough tragedy of 1989, which was when a series of failures by the police led to the deaths of ninety-six people, yet the authorities at the time blamed football supporters for the tragedy.

It is novel, Barkan posits, that political leaders draw attention to the wrongs committed by governments or institutions of their societies in the past. Previously, society did not in general look back so much – or at least so regretfully; when it did look back, the tales it told of itself to itself tended to be myths of past greatness. This is especially true for Conservative prime ministers; indeed when in office Mr. Cameron was particularly fond of the phrase the 'bad old days', using it on a number of occasions, but most notably in 2012 in relation to kicking out racism in football.[8] Someone in his position, the most senior member of the Conservative party, would have once preferred the 'good old days'. National myths about nations have tended to be based on heroic deeds and victory. The kings and great leaders would take centre stage and those that they governed were either portrayed as happy and grateful, or not mentioned at all. Those myths were one-sided;

---

[6] D. Lowenthal, *The Heritage Crusade and the Spoils of History* (Cambridge, 1998); and also *The Past is a Foreign Country* (Cambridge, 1995).

[7] Elazar Barkan, *The Guilt of Nations: Restitution and Negotiating Historical Injustices* (Baltimore, Md., 2001), p. 316.

[8] 'David Cameron calls football racism summit', *The Guardian,* 12 Feb. 2012.

they celebrated the elite of a culture – the victors; the losers were brushed aside. The new collective memory that is being forged, by contrast, is one more likely to recognize the heinous rather than the heroic, the victims over the victorious. It is curious that this development is a top down as much as – if not more so than – a bottom-up phenomenon.

This turn towards the worst aspects of the past is evident in the museums built in recent decades. In the past thirty years, more memorial museums have opened than in the previous 100 years. These include the memorial museum of the 9/11 attacks; sixteen Holocaust museums in the U.S. alone (with plans for more); and a museum dedicated to those who died and lost their loved ones in the bombing in Oklahoma City in 1995. There are scores of museums documenting slavery in America, and genocide in Armenia, Rwanda and the Balkans. Others show state repression in Eastern Europe; apartheid in South Africa; political 'disappearances' in Argentina; and massacres in China and Taiwan. Even within older institutions, such as the Natural History Museum in London, there is a memorial, alongside the natural history specimens and the old dinosaurs, to the lives lost in 2004 when an earthquake in the Indian Ocean caused a tsunami that led to the deaths of around 300,000 people, including British holiday-makers in Thailand. In institutions that used to valorize great deeds and achievements of human civilization, this is a significant departure.

It came from within

The inclination to repatriate objects, or grant a sympathetic ear to the possibility, often comes from *within* museums and the academy, either because its members proactively attempt to solicit repatriation requests, or because they are unable to argue firmly a defence for retention when they receive them, effectively advertizing for repatriation claims.[9] Take the dynamics of the claim to return the Okukor. The demand for the return of the cockerel came, not from people in Nigeria, though Nigeria has long appealed for the return of bronzes, if not the Okukor, but from students within Cambridge University. A similar pattern of events took place with a related controversy, which was set alight one month before that of the cockerel.

High up on the façade of Oriel College in the High Street of Oxford, stands – for now – a small statue of Cecil John Rhodes, the Victorian imperialist who shaped Britain's empire in Africa and who, in 1887, told

---

[9] See T. Jenkins, *Keeping their Marbles: how the Treasures of the Past Ended Up in Museums – And Why They Should Stay There* (Oxford, 2016), for an in-depth examination of this dynamic.

the house of assembly in Cape Town that 'The native is to be treated as a child and denied the franchise'.[10] In the autumn of 2015 students at Oriel College, led by a South African Rhodes Scholar, Ntokozo Qwabe, kick-started what became known as the 'Rhodes Must Fall' campaign, arguing that the statue of Rhodes should be removed. Rhodes had studied at Oriel, intermittently, between 1873 and 1881, and bequeathed funds to the college in his will. To the university he left the legacy that founded the Rhodes Scholarships: it is this money that funded the students who wanted his statue removed.

The campaign had its origins at the University of Cape Town in South Africa, where Rhodes built his fortune and power before his death in 1902 and where there was a statue honouring his legacy. In March 2015, activist Chumani Maxwele smeared excrement on the statue, triggering further protests by activists who complained that the statue had 'great symbolic power' which glorified someone 'who exploited black labour and stole land from indigenous people'[11] and should be taken down. In a short space of time they were successful: one month after the protests began, the university authorities removed the statue. The campaign then spread like wildfire to America and Europe where different groups, especially on university campuses, argued that statues including those of Thomas Jefferson, the third American president, and of Jefferson Davis, the president of the Confederacy during the Civil War, be toppled.

In one respect, it's hard to get all that excited either way about a small statue of a Victorian imperialist. There are lots of monuments to old white men all over the world, men whose influence and often names have been forgotten, and whose time has passed. Unlike many of the contested artefacts in museums or universities, as with the cockerel, the statues are political and unremarkable; neither pretty to look at nor unique evidence of past peoples' ways of living. It's possible they educate passers-by about the tangled web of history they pass, but more often than not, they are forgotten. We might not even notice their absence: I grew up in Oxford and only noticed the statue of Rhodes once the campaign drew it to my attention. Even so, this controversy and the future of such statues is important because of the claims that are made for removing old pieces of stone: primarily, that it is a necessary part of repairing the past, akin to decolonization.

Decolonization, which took place in the second half of the twentieth century, was driven by the great social movements that swept through

---

[10] Cited in R. L. Rotberg, *The Founder: Cecil Rhodes and the Pursuit of Power* (Oxford, 1998), p. 225.'

[11] Rhodes statue removed in Cape Town as crowd celebrates', *B.B.C. News*, 8 Apr. 2015 <http://www.bbc.com/news/world-africa-32236922> [accessed 17 Apr. 2018].

Africa and Asia and forcefully challenged the might of European rule. They grew out of the insistence that people of Africa and Asia could and should run their own lives and be free from the domination of Europe, challenging Rhodes's argument that they were to be treated like children, or worse. To compare this major transformation which came out of many years of hard struggle to what might be brought about through the removal of a statue is to elide two very different movements and achievements. And in so doing, there is a danger that it diminishes the earlier battles and even the meaning of 'decolonization'.

It is true that toppling statues has been at the heart of significant political and social change. During the Protestant Reformation, Catholic statues were defaced and destroyed; during the French revolution statues of monarchs and their artworks were demolished; in post-independence India, statues of viceroys and British monarchs were taken down and neutered by placing them in Delhi's Coronation Park. But in all these cases the toppling of statues came as part of a great social upheaval or in the midst of great change when the old oppressive regime also was removed. The 'Rhodes Must Fall' formed a long time after decolonization, and – not insignificantly – in a time of political *in*action, where removing statues appears to stand in for social change. As the author of *The Meaning of Race*, Kenan Malik, observed in an article on *Aljazeera*: 'Once upon a time, student activists used to demand that capitalism must fall, or that apartheid must be crushed, or that colonialism must be swept away. Now, it seems, they just want to take down statues'.[12] This is one of the limits to such campaigns and, indeed, repatriation: that it stands in for social change, that it does little to advance material and political equality, and that statues and museum objects are expected to do more work than they can achieve, turning the latter into objects of apology where they were once objects of enlightenment.

We must organize to mourn – the end of politics

In *Making Whole What Has Been Smashed: on Reparations Politics,* the sociologist John Torpey analyses the trends towards apologies, reparations, and repatriations, and is especially interested in explaining what he describes as the 'avalanche' of such activity that has taken place post-1989. Torpey suggests that the increasing efforts to make amends have arisen at the same time as forward-looking, future-oriented political movements have been in decline. In short, he argues that reparations thinking arose in the face

[12] K. Malik, 'The Cecil Rhodes statue is not the problem', *Al Jazeera*, 11 Jan. 2016 <http://www.aljazeera.com/indepth/opinion/2016/01/cecil-rhodes-oxford-problem-160110061336569.html> [accessed 17 Apr. 2018].

of political defeat. It is, he writes, 'a substitute for expansive visions of an alternative human future of the kind that animated the socialist movements of the preceding century, which have been overwhelmingly discredited since the fall of the Berlin Wall in 1989'.[13] What he means is that developments that include the end of the Cold War and the collapse of an 'alternative' politics – by which he means any form of socialist movement – have transformed contemporary politics, making it less about competing social visions for the future and more about accepting and managing the status quo.

Torpey argues that it is difficult to overstate the significance of this change in outlook. Over the past two centuries, the big projects that captured the attention and focus of society were capitalism, socialism and the idea of democracy. Even when people were at loggerheads, or at war – be that the Soviet Union against the U.S.A., capitalism versus communism, battles over extending the franchise to wider sections of the population, or fights about extending democracy to new nations – Torpey posits that society was driven by visions of how things could be, or should be. They were future orientated. Today, he contends, these aspirations have been found wanting and to a great extent, abandoned. Utopia is considered a dangerous aim.

From the 1970s onwards, political movements weakened and shrank. The slogan popularized by Conservative prime minister Margaret Thatcher to underline the defeat of socialist economics – that 'There Is No Alternative' to the free market and economic liberalism – is now generally accepted. The competing political sides of 'Left' and 'Right', which were formed in the times of the French Revolution, now compete over the centre ground. People continue to protest, and agitate for change, but in a way that is more inchoate, less directed, less effective, and less popular. And it is oriented far more around the process of the present day – or the wrongs of the past – than around visions of the future.

As visions of a transformed future seem less plausible, people have turned away from fighting for the good society. And in this context, the past has become a battleground. For Torpey, the desire to atone for past wrongs has come to supplant the search for a better tomorrow; the demand for reparations has supplanted the fight for a future. He recalls a phrase that was used within the socialist and labour movements – 'Don't mourn, organise' – which, he notes, has been replaced by a sensibility that urges us instead to 'organise to mourn', ushering in what he calls the 'politics of tears'.[14] The political theorist Wendy Brown draws similar conclusions, characterizing the

---

[13] J. Torpey, *Making Whole What Has Been Smashed: on Reparations Politics* (Cambridge, Mass., 2006), p. 16.

[14] Torpey, *Making Whole What Has Been Smashed*, p. 1.

turn towards the recognition of victimhood – a key demand in reparations politics – as 'the language of unfreedom': 'its impulse to inscribe in the law and in other political registers its historical and present pain rather than conjure an imagined future of power to make itself'.[15] In this regard, it is argued, campaigners focus on reparations and the recognition of damage instead of shaping the life they would like to lead.

Who benefits?

Repatriation, restitution and reparations, are all presented as positive for the victims of historic wrongs. It is assumed that the people of the countries to which the objects would be returned, or those who receive reparation, will benefit. But this assumption is questionable.

When Elazar Barkan documented the rise of restitution cases in the 1990s, he was intrigued that pressure for restitution and apology was more likely to come from the perceived perpetrators than from the victims. And the fact that political leaders seemed to be driving the process was of interest to him. Why would they invite such demands for reparations? Barkan thus explored the alleged perpetrators' willingness to engage and accommodate to the alleged victims' demands. Especially from the 1990s onwards, he identified a 'new world opinion in which appearing compassionate and holding the moral high ground has become a good investment'. Barkan concluded that reparations are acts that bring moral credibility to the elites of today, by drawing a contrast with the morally dubious actions of their predecessors. The political philosopher Jean Bethke Elshtain describes apologies from political leaders and institutions as 'contrition chic': 'a bargain-basement way to gain publicity, sympathy, and even absolution [that] now extends to entire nations'.[16] While these critics may seem a little harsh, there is no doubt that the processes they identify – making some kind of apologetic gesture – can act to secure legitimation for leaders.

It can also be used as an excuse for not doing things today. Consider what energy and ideas are now diverted away from imagining a better future when those who would have fought for it are now so distracted by finding the cause of present problems predominantly in the past. This is a point that the writer Marina Warner makes, in an essay on the ritual of public apologies: 'Yes, well, what are you doing about us now?'[17]

---

[15] W. Brown, *States of Injury: Power and Freedom in Late Modernity* (Princeton, N.J., 1995), p. 66.

[16] J. Bethke Elshtain, 'Politics and forgiveness', in *Burying the Past: Making Peace and Doing Justice After Civil Conflict,* ed. N. Biggar (Georgetown, D.C., 2003), p. 45.

[17] M. Warner, 'Sorry: the present state of apology', *Open Democracy* (7 Nov. 2002).

Even if we accept that today's political elites have something to gain from the rhetoric of reparations, is it not the case that the victims gain something too? Here, too, questions need to be asked. Theorists raise legitimate concerns about the way people are seen when their role is deemed to be simply that of the victim of historical wrongs. The one-sided presentation of the loser of a conflict as one whose life and that of their descendants is invariably damaged can rewrite the role that people actually played in the shaping of their circumstances. Those who fought and struggled, and whose actions had an impact, are recast in a passive role, as simply having been on the receiving end of violence and injustice. Elizabeth Willis, an emeritus curator at Museums Victoria in Melbourne, Australia, makes this observation, even though she broadly supports campaigns for reconciliation and the recognition of past wrongs by the repatriation of artefacts. Willis's research into the case of Aboriginal populations found that reparations, even repatriation claims, tend to ignore the agency of these people, simplifying and reducing the role they played. These claims 'can, unwittingly, diminish people', she observes, recasting people who fought as merely injured parties who suffered and failed.[18]

As well as rewriting a more complicated history, the impact of emphasizing the victimhood of groups may have negative implications for how people are encouraged to view themselves today. People are presented, and asked to perceive themselves, as defined only by what heinous things were done to their ancestors. They are identified as having a history of frailty, and as being now reliant on their conquerors to bestow upon them some kind of compensation. This fatalistic view sees the people of today as forever imprisoned by a past that pre-dates their own existence, and encourages them to find refuge in enduring victimhood. In order to bid for reparations or compensation, different groups have to compete over how much they suffered, and this in turn helps to shape a culture of grievance.

The movement for reparations is an example of a trend which relies on therapeutic measures, such as the recognition of historic ills through the removal of cultural artefacts, as a way to solve social problems. But in the process of making claims, groups and individuals have to enter a competition in which their wounds are evaluated. They cannot just ask for money, or demand material and political equality; rather, they have to prove how badly they have been affected. Because of this competitive dynamic, reparations are more likely to divide than reconcile. And because the process relies on supplication, with the victim asking the historical

---

[18] E. Willis, 'The law, politics, and "historical wounds": the Dja Dja Warrung Bark Etchings case in Australia', *International Jour. Cultural Property*, xv (2008), 49–63.

victor for a hand-out or a statement of recognition, power relations are not transformed, but reinforced.

We also have to look at what the idea of reparations says about descendants of the so-called perpetrators of historical wrongs. People living today, most of whom were born long after the event in question, are held culpable for the past – not because of their own actions, but because of the particular national, religious, ethnic, or racial group to which they belong. Thus it is said that British people today, and their institutions, are responsible for the suffering of those people conquered and subjected by the British empire, and should assume a sense of collective guilt for the sins of imperialism. This has uncomfortable echoes with old racializing discourse, which promoted notions about the biological inheritance of moral traits, and the culpability of whole populations or groups for the actions of their ancestors.

Finally, by presenting the people of today as casualties of the past, the move towards reparations implicitly detaches responsibility for action in the *present*. By encouraging people to blame the past for today's troubles, rather than face up to the problems of the present and future, the all-important relationship between action and accountability becomes eroded.

Rewriting history

The American attorney Alan Audi states:

> From an anti-imperial [*sic*] perspective, I believe that the starting point must be restitution. Simply put, a wrongfully taken object should be returned, including objects taken by virtue of an imperial, exploitative apparatus that is widely abhorred today.[19]

The journalist Henry Porter ventures that for a similar reason, the Elgin Marbles should be sent back to Greece:

> To weigh the issue, you need only ask yourself if Elgin's behaviour would be acceptable today. Of course it wouldn't, and nor would we expect to keep the result of such looting. So why do we hold on to these ill-gotten sculptures now?[20]

Examining and reassessing the past is something that museums and historians do all the time, and rightly so. But these commentators are calling for something quite different: an exercise in reading history backwards, judging it by a particular set of contemporary mores, and then taking action

---

[19] A. Audi, 'A semiotics of cultural property argument', *International Jour. Cultural Property*, xiv (2007), 131–56.

[20] H. Porter, 'The Greeks gave us the Olympics. Let them have their marbles', *The Observer*, 20 May 2012.

on the basis of how we – or rather, a number of influential commentators – feel about it now.

Attempting to undo history in this way erodes the differences between historical periods. Interpreting history through the eyes of the present contorts our understanding of what happened and why, and reduces what is always a more complex picture, in the interests of making us feel better. The first step in understanding the past is to appreciate that things have not always been the same; that many of the actions that appear unjust, even monstrous, to the present-day sensibility were accepted norms at the time. It is far better to try to get to grips with the past, and understand what gave rise to certain values and practices, than to embark on a futile project of trying to undo it.

Besides, where would such actions stop? And who decides? History is long and untidy. It is always more complicated than the goodies versus the baddies. If we take the two cases of the Parthenon marbles and the Benin bronzes, both subject to claims for return on the basis of historical wrongs, we find a tangled path. The ancient Athenians were not angels, but warriors. The Parthenon was a display of power and it was built by slaves; the enemies of the Athenian empire would quite rightly have seen it as a monument to their humiliation. The glory of Benin was built on the slave trade: the contested Benin bronzes were crafted from manillas, brought by European traders, traded for slaves, and melted down.[21] In some instances, then, the very sculptures and plaques that some would like to see returned to Nigeria were made from the proceeds of slavery, exchanged for men and women. Are these artefacts tainted by how the material was created and acquired?

Judging the past though the eyes of the present does not change what happened. Nor will it aid our understanding of ancient Athens, nineteenth-century Europe, or Benin during its golden age. The best way to respect the lives of the people who came before us is to research history without such an agenda.

Throughout history, harm has been done; but it cannot be 'repaired', only studied and understood. The obsession with museums and their 'loot' can mean that we avoid engaging with the deeper forces that brought about war, colonization and imperialism; we focus on objects and museums as the source of domination, rather than seeing them as institutions and artefacts that reflect wider political and social events of their times. In asking artefacts to atone for the past, we lose sight of their original meanings and purposes, viewing them only as objects of tragedy and apology. This hampers our appreciation of the artefacts; what they meant to their creators and owners, and what they say about their moment of origin.

---

[21] Manillas were a West African metallic currency in the form of armlets.

9. British universities and Caribbean slavery

Nicholas Draper

Implicit in the title of the colloquium on which this volume is based – 'History, Heritage and Ideology' – is a declension: I/we do history; you do heritage; they do ideology. This was not intentional, I am sure. But it is the more revealing for that. 'They' – the unpaid historians and community activists who are held to do ideology – were not there with us in the room, which comprised academic historians, heritage professionals and university administrators. I do not represent the 'they', but I do speak to some of them. And I can report that there is mounting anger over the ways in which universities – and not only universities – are failing to deal with their histories of entanglement with British colonial slavery as one component of Britain's wider colonial past. David Cannadine has suggested that this anger flowed from an infantile fury at the discovery that the past was often cruel and violent.[1] I do not think this is correct. The anger flows from the continued complacent and uncritical representation and celebration of that often cruel and violent past as progressive, liberal, enlightened. Unless there are changes in approach, unless universities lead in the research and exploration of their own histories, there is likely to be increased polarization between inside and outside groups, growing frustration on both sides and ultimately the eruption of destructive conflicts in which universities, driven onto the back foot, impugn the legitimacy of their critics and further entrench versions of themselves that reject the values of evidence-based analysis and of engagement with society which supposedly they embody.

It does not have to be this way. The experience of the U.S. shows not only what happens when universities remain passive until the storm breaks over their heads (for example, the recent conflicts at Georgetown and Yale[2]), but also what can be achieved by universities taking on the responsibility

---

[1] See D. Cannadine, 'Introduction' above, pp. 8–9.

[2] 'Yale grapples with ties to slavery in debate over a college's name', *The New York Times* <https://www.nytimes.com/2015/09/12/nyregion/yale-in-debate-over-calhoun-college-grapples-with-ties-to-slavery.html?_r=0> [accessed 3 Aug. 2017]; Georgetown University, 'Georgetown apologizes for 1838 sale of 272 slaves, dedicates buildings' <https://www.georgetown.edu/news/liturgy-remembrance-contrition-hope-slavery> [accessed 7 Aug. 2017]; C. S. Wilder, *Ebony and Ivy* (2013).

N. Draper, 'British universities and Caribbean slavery', in *Dethroning historical reputations: universities, museums and the commemoration of benefactors*, ed. J. Pellew and L. Goldman (2018), pp. 93–107.

for their own history. The process undertaken by Brown under Ruth Simmons more than a decade ago, and which among other thing led to the establishment of the 'Center for the Study of Slavery and Justice' under Tony Bogue, appears exemplary in this context.[3]

Universities and other institutions in Britain[4] might well respond that yes, they can see a problem in the U.S., where slavery was embedded, but Britain was (and remains) in a different position, with slavery having been purely a colonial phenomenon, with no history of chattel slavery in the metropole. Distance certainly insulated metropolitan Britain from the realities of slavery in the past, but that distantiation is unlikely to save universities today, because of course slavery came home to Britain, and to British higher education, in many different ways. And universities are especially powerful sites for the analysis of 'the debt to slavery': if institutions which in their values and aspirations appear to represent the antithesis of the slave-system owe their existence, maintenance or growth to that system, what does that mean for our collective assumptions about Britain's liberal past? And what does it mean for our present if universities continue to ignore the parts of their history that are less convenient, or to deny the relevance of these pasts?

If work is to be undertaken by British universities on their linkages with slavery, it will need to be both precise and comprehensive about the nature of such linkages: those were the objectives and the methods of the Brown report. A comprehensive account of connections to slavery for any British institution would encompass not only its linkages to slave-ownership but also its relationship with the financial, cultural and physical legacies of the concentric circles of involvement centred on the slave-economy: the slave-trade and slave-traders; the supply and fitting out of slave-trade vessels; the supply of trade goods for West Africa; the export of manufactures to the slave-colonies themselves; the commodity flows in sugar, tobacco and other goods produced by enslaved Africans; the financial structures and institutions, the development of which was in whole or in part a function of the slave-economy; and, perhaps most potently of all, the intellectual formations surrounding 'race' which were formed and re-formed in the era of British colonial slavery and its aftermath.

The Legacies of British Slave-ownership project (L.B.S.), and the evidence it provides, is focused on the owners of enslaved Africans and on

---

[3] Brown University, *Slavery and Justice, Report of the Brown University Steering Committee on Slavery and Justice* <http://www.brown.edu/Research/Slavery_Justice> [accessed 3 Aug. 2017].

[4] This paper is confined to England, Scotland and Wales, and does not consider universities in Ireland, although the Legacies of British Slaveholding project itself does embrace slave-owners in Ireland.

the immediate financial claims of mortgagees and legatees secured on the bodies and lives of the enslaved and their unborn children. It thus represents only one piece of a much bigger picture. But the evidence we are building, of who actually owned or mortgaged enslaved people in the period from *c.*1763 to 1834, can be used as a start-point for tabling the kinds of issues raised more broadly by slavery for the histories of our British universities. Conventionally, the focus in such explorations is on benefactors – Eric Williams famously foregrounded the case of the Codrington Library at All Souls as an example.[5] Founders and benefactors are indeed central. But in this paper I intend to raise also three other possible types of linkage between universities and slave-ownership: universities themselves as slave-owners; what would now be called 'faculty members' as slave-owners; and students as slave-owners. In no way is this intended as a comprehensive survey. Instead, it focuses on a number of cases that have been discovered or highlighted in L.B.S.'s work to date, effectively as a by-product of our research. We have not set out to investigate British universities specifically: instead, we have logged the instances in which universities appear in the findings of our broader cataloguing of British slave-ownership.

Founders and benefactors as slave-owners

Founders, either as prime movers in the organization of a wider effort to establish new educational institutions or as funders of such establishments, appear to create an especially intimate linkage between a university and a given form of wealth, the very existence of that institution being embedded in the material interests of its founders. By definition, the oldest Scottish universities (St. Andrews, Aberdeen, Edinburgh and Glasgow), and Oxford and Cambridge, founded before the inception of British colonial slavery, lie outside this category, but the universities founded in the eighteenth and the early nineteenth century potentially fall into this analysis. With the broadening of tertiary education in the Victorian period, the question arises as to what extent and in what ways slave-ownership can be relevant to these institutions, established after the end of British colonial slavery in 1838.

King's College London, founded in 1828 as an Anglican response to the godless 'London University' (now University College London) and granted a Royal Charter in 1829, raised funds through soliciting donations and by selling shares of £100 each, and its linkages to slavery can be explored through an analysis of the lists of donors and subscribers. The initial core funding came from the Anglican hierarchy led by the archbishop of Canterbury and

⁵ E. Williams, *Capitalism and Slavery* (Chapel Hill, N.C., 1994 [1944]), p. 90.

the bishop of London, who gave £1,000 each: these senior clerics were not slave-owners, although as is widely known the Society for the Propagation of the Gospel in Foreign Parts founded by their predecessors owned the Codrington estates on Barbados and the enslaved people upon them. But the wider subscription lists included (alongside William Wilberforce, who gave £50) more than fifty slave-owners and as many again who were linked to slave-ownership as trustees, agents or family members. Among the former were John Gladstone (a major slave-owner in British Guiana, and purchaser of one share of £100); John Bolton (the Liverpool slave-owner and slave-trader, responsible for shipping more than 20,000 enslaved Africans across the Atlantic, who gave £100); and the alderman and M.P. John Atkins (who owned more than 500 men, women and children in Jamaica and who gave £100 and subscribed for two shares of £100). In a signal of financial pressures on Jamaica slave-owners in the last years of slavery, Charles Nicholas Pallmer M.P. for Surrey, previously chairman of the 'Standing Committee of the West India Planters and Merchants' lobbying group between 1818 and 1820 and owner of hundreds of enslaved people in Jamaica, made a donation of £100 and paid the first part of his subscription to five shares of £100 but then appears to have reneged on the £475 balance of his subscription. Of the 907 individuals who gave over £50 or bought at least one share of £100, some 7 per cent were close enough to the slave-economy to appear in the slave compensation records.[6] These also included as an annual subscriber of £5, Henry Phillpotts, then dean of Chester and later the bishop of Exeter (whose subscription fell into arrears), often characterized misleadingly as a slave-owner: in fact he was trustee for the earl of Dudley, who was himself a subscriber to University College London and who owned at his death in 1833 some 665 enslaved people on three estates in Jamaica. Although the earl of Dudley was not representative of the founders of U.C.L., either in his aristocratic status or in his slave-ownership, their number also included John Smith, of the banking firm of Smith, Payne & Smith, which lent heavily to the West India merchant firm of Manning & Anderdon (whose senior partner William Manning, subscribed to one £100 share in King's College

[6] N. Draper, *The Price of Emancipation* (Cambridge, 2010), pp. 331–4 shows 76 individual subscribers and donors who appeared in the records of the Commissioners of Slave Compensation, of whom five were only tentatively identified as the same person in the two sets of data. A more definitive subsequent review based on 'List of donation and subscriptions of £100 each' in *The Statement of Proceedings Towards the Establishment of King's College 1830* (1830), pp. 57–95 appears in M. Watson, 'The imprint of slavery on London: King's College London' (unpublished University College London M.A. thesis, 2014). The underlying work for this thesis showed an adjusted total of 105 donors and subscribers (out of 1489) sufficiently connected with the slave-economy to appear in the compensation records.

London). Manning & Anderdon had itself become intensely engaged in the slave-economy: to date, we have found sixteen separate estates with over 1,500 enslaved people of which the firm was owner, lessee or mortgagee-in-possession between the abolition of the slave-trade and the abolition of slavery. When Manning & Anderdon failed in 1831, Smith Payne & Smith moved to secure its exposure by seizing estates and enslaved people and mortgages over estates and enslaved people, becoming prominent claimants in the slave compensation process of the 1830s.

Universities founded in the later Victorian era, after the end of slavery, pose different questions in their relationship to slave-ownership (and to slavery more widely). At Liverpool, key early physical developments included:

> A large engineering laboratory (the gift of Sir A. B. Walker, 1889); the main Victoria building, including a fine library presented by Sir Henry Tate, and the clock tower erected from the civic subscription to commemorate the jubilee of 1887 (opened 1892); magnificent laboratories of physiology and pathology, given by Rev. S. A. Thompson Yates (opened 1895); and a handsome botanical laboratory given by Mr. W. P. Hartley (1902).[7]

The name of Sir Henry Tate draws reflexive responses connecting him with slavery. He was an adolescent when British colonial slavery ended, so the connection must lie in (1) his sourcing (if such there was) of slave-grown sugar in other European colonies after British emancipation; and/or (2) his more general exploitation of patterns of production and demand in the sugar market, undoubtedly established through slavery in the two centuries prior to his birth. Either or both of these might be valid: but Tate was certainly was not a slave-owner or descended from them. The connection to slave-ownership for the University of Liverpool in this context runs in fact through S. A. Thompson Yates, who was born S. A. Thompson, the son of Samuel Henry Thompson (1807–92) and Elizabeth Yates (1815–92). Elizabeth Yates in turn was the eldest daughter of Joseph Brooks Yates. The *O.D.N.B.* says of Joseph Brooks Yates:

> After leaving Eton about 1796, he joined the firm of a West Indies merchant, in which he became a partner, remaining with it until shortly before he died. He was one of the leading reformers of Liverpool, and in the years after 1815 was a prominent figure in local campaigns and petitions in favour of civil liberties, adherence to constitutional rights, and democratic reform. He was also a liberal

---

[7] 'Liverpool: the University', in *Victoria County History of Lancaster*: iv. 53–4, available on *British History Online* <http://www.british-history.ac.uk/vch/lancs/vol4/pp53-54> [accessed 21 Apr. 2018].

supporter of the city's literary and scientific institutions. In February 1812 he joined with Thomas Stewart Traill in founding the Liverpool Literary and Philosophical Society, of which he was president for a total of twelve years. He was president of the Liverpool Royal Institution in 1842–3, and was also one of the founders of the Southern and Toxteth Hospital at Liverpool.[8]

All this is true but Yates also owned or held mortgages over 1,000 enslaved people at the time of Emancipation. It is his name that is carried and perpetuated by the building, and possibly his money that in part funded it. S. A. Thompson Yates's mother was co-heiress of her father, inheriting one-fifth of Joseph Brook Yates's estate, while her husband Samuel Henry Thompson was executor of Yates's will. Samuel Henry Thompson himself died a millionaire in 1892: he (as was his father before him) was a long-term partner in the banking firm of Heywood & Co. (a predecessor of Barclays), a bank founded by the Heywood brothers, 'experienced in the African trade', as the history of the bank puts it – they were slave-traders. Without access to the family financial records – and Checkland's biography of the Gladstones appears unique among histories of slave-owning families in the clarity with which it could set out the building of the family fortune – it is not possible to specify the extent of the flow of wealth to S. A. Thompson Yates from Joseph Brooks Yates's slave-ownership, as opposed to the flow from a banking business founded on the slave-trade. But in either case there appears to be a possible issue posed by the name of the Thompson Yates Building, which remains part of the University of Liverpool.

The history of the University of Liverpool goes on to say:

> During the same period [1889–1902] eight additional chairs were endowed, and many lectureships and scholarships were founded. Throughout the early history of the college it had rested mainly on the support of a comparatively small group of friends; among those whose munificence rendered possible the rapid development of the college, special mention should be made, in addition to those already named, of the fifteenth and sixteenth Earls of Derby, successive presidents of the college, both of whom founded chairs; of Mr. George Holt, most princely of the early benefactors; of Sir John Brunner, Mr. Holbrook Gaskell, and Mr. Thomas Harrison, all of whom founded chairs; and of Mr. E. K. Muspratt, Mr. John Rankin, Mr. J. W. Alsop, Mr. A. F. Warr, Mr. C. W. Jones, Sir Edward Lawrence.[9]

---

[8] C. W. Sutton (rev. A G Crosby), 'Yates, Joseph Brooks (1780–1858)', in *O.D.N.B.* <https://doi.org/10.1093/ref:odnb/30195> [accessed 29 May 2018].

[9] 'Liverpool: the university', pp. 53–4.

Names on this last list highlight some of the commercial connections of Liverpool to the slave-economy beyond slave-ownership. George Holt was a shipping magnate, as were his brothers Alfred and Philip. The three men were sons of a major cotton broker, also named George Holt who died in 1861 and whose trade in that period was by definition in slave-grown cotton from the southern U.S. Sir Edward Lawrence, who died in 1909, was a director of the Anglo-Confederate Trading Co. in the era of the American Civil War. In 1862 he registered the blockade-runner *Banshee* in the name of Edward Lawrence & Co. and in 1863 the blockade runner *Wild Dayrell* for the Anglo-Confederate Trading Co.[10]

For British universities, the circle of benefactors will be much larger than that of founders. Every university extant in the eighteenth and early nineteenth century is likely to have received gifts derived from slavery. Eric Williams's example of the Codrington Library is re-used repeatedly – and it is indeed a powerful expression of the connection of civilization and barbarism – but it is not an isolated example, instead representing a wider phenomenon whose scale at present remains unknown, because gifts that are less spectacular than the Codrington Library are not always – or indeed not often – visible from the outside, although cumulatively they might dwarf it in importance. It is only because in the course of L.B.S.'s work we have reviewed his will that we know, for example, that John Dawkins, a fellow of All Souls for almost fifty years, a forebear of Professor Richard Dawkins and the owner of 475 enslaved men, women and children in Trelawney, Jamaica, left 200 guineas to All Souls at his death in 1844. In the absence of work by the beneficiary institutions themselves, it is not possible to get a handle on the true extent and significance of such gifts: and the risk arises that assumptions are made that in fact overstate the importance of this giving.

Some similar gifts are known. Eric Williams highlighted the Hibbert Trust, as it became known, that among other things offered divinity scholarships. Candidates would only be considered if their degree came from an institution such as London University 'where degrees were granted without subscription to the articles of religion'. The trust was funded by Robert Hibbert in 1847 with U.S. $50,000 in Ohio stock and £8,000 in railway shares. Hibbert had petitioned parliament in 1833 opposing Emancipation, even with compensation for his 560 enslaved people, whom he valued at £70,000: the emancipation plan he said would be 'utterly ruinous to himself, and to others who are similarly situated'.[11]

---

[10] J. McKenna, *British Ships in the Confederate Navy* (Jefferson, N.C., 2010), p. 213; *Liverpool Post*, 14 Dec. 1863.

[11] J. Murch, *Memoir of Robert Hibbert, Founder of the Hibbert Trust: with a Sketch of its History* (Bath, 1874); A. R. Ruston, *The Hibbert Trust: a History* (1984).

At St. David's Lampeter (now University of Wales Trinity St. David), the Phillips Collection comprises over 22,500 books donated from 1834 onwards by Thomas Phillips; he also endowed six scholarships, left St. David's shares in the London & Westminster banks worth £7,000, and established in his will a chair of natural science there. Phillips has an entry in the *O.D.N.B.* as 'philanthropist and surgeon' that describes his career in India and – interestingly – at Botany Bay. What it does not say is that this Nabob had invested part of his imperial wealth in buying the Camden Park estate and enslaved people attached to it on St. Vincent, reportedly for over £40,000, *c.* 1820, or that he then purchased and moved a further eighty-five enslaved people from Cariacou to the estate, or that the number of enslaved people on the estate declined from 231 in 1822 to 164 at the time of compensation, with fifty-five deaths (one quarter of the enslaved population) recorded between 1822 and 1825 and another thirty-nine deaths (a further one quarter) between 1825 and 1828.

Where connections are recognized, the reading of some of the philanthropic legacies can reproduce a culture of abolitionism in which slavery is elided. At Aberdeen, Hugh Fraser Leslie reportedly commissioned the building of the Powis Gates in 1834. According to an Aberdeen University walking tour:

> Turn left along the High Street and, about 50 yards down, pause to look across the street at this imposing gateway. This has no original link with King's but was erected in 1834 by Hugh Fraser Leslie of Powis – the lively owner of a straggling estate lying to the West of Old Aberdeen. The minaret towers of the structure may suggest a Turkish influence. Above the arch is the coat of arms of the Fraser Leslie family. Another shield at the back carries busts of three black slaves, commemorating the family's link with the grant of freedom to the slaves on their Jamaica plantations. Mr. Leslie's fantasy gates may have been designed to underline his view that he was as important as the College.[12]

Hugh Fraser Leslie had managed his own estates in Jamaica in the 1830s and campaigned for further compensation for the early end of Apprenticeship of formerly enslaved field workers in 1838, having described anti-slavery campaigners as 'the washings and scrapings of the manufacturing districts'.[13]

Universities as slave-owners

Perhaps the most vividly damaging connection in the U.S. has been with the ownership and sale of enslaved people by the universities themselves, a

---

[12] <https://www.abdn.ac.uk/events/documents/history.pdf> [accessed 2 Aug. 2017].
[13] 'West India Emancipation in 1838', *Anti-slavery Examiner, Omnibus*, x. 62.

history recently surfacing at Georgetown. To date we have no evidence of direct ownership of enslaved people by universities or colleges in Britain, in contrast to other institutions such as the Society for the Propagation of the Gospel in Foreign Parts or Greenwich Hospital. But a word of caution is in order here. The slave compensation records, one of our major archival sources, show individuals rather than institutions. Hence, as noted above, the Society for the Propagation of the Gospel was compensated through its treasurer, James Heywood Markland (who also was active in anti-abolition campaigning as a member of the Literary Committee of the Society of West India Merchants and Planters in the 1820s). So institutions may lie behind individual names of slave-owners. One award that has aroused our interest in this context, although there is no direct evidence to date that it is indeed such a case, is the Revd. John Wilson, who had been senior bursar of Queen's College Oxford in 1830–1 and 1831–2 and was junior bursar in 1832–3, when he bought Olivees and the more than 100 enslaved people on the estate in St. Kitts, for whom he was compensated as 'Rev. John Wilson of Queen's College Oxford' in 1835.[14]

In another case, a contingent legacy appears not to have been triggered. John Lawrence Aikenhead matriculated Trinity College, Oxford, on 14 May 1752 aged 17, took a B.C.L. in 1759, and a D.C.L. 8th July 1773. Aikenhead had inherited the Stirling Castle estate and the enslaved people attached to it in Jamaica from his father William in 1760. When he himself died in 1780 he left Stirling Castle and the enslaved people attached to it to his second son, also named William, with annuities to his wife and daughters chargeable upon it; in default of issue it would pass to Robert Graham and his heirs, then to Robert Hamilton and his heirs, and in default of any of the above to be sold by Trinity College Oxford to (re)build the College according to the plans by Sir Christopher Wren 'as also' to buy up houses to enlarge college garden, and if Trinity declined to take on the trust the estate was to be sold by the City of Bath to construct 'a more elegant and extensive pump room, public room ... in the Lower Town of Bath' under the design or direction of 'Mr. Wyatt'. With such a chain of contingencies, it was unlikely that Trinity would have inherited the enslaved people.

---

[14] In his will, proved 30/12/1857, after the end of slavery, when he was Rector of Holwell, Revd. John Wilson left his residuary estate in trust for the benefit of his wife and then her sisters, and then to the provost and fellows of Queen's College Oxford to be applied by them 'to the encouragement of theological learning and preparation for the Christian ministry among the undergraduates of the College in their fourth years' standing and Bachelors of Arts in their first years' standing by instituting prizes for the greatest proficiency to be ascertained by written essays or public examinations in the College Hall' or by other means (PROB 11/2262/383).

'Faculty members' as slave-owners

Universities and their constituent bodies construct their histories in part through their commemoration and celebration of select individuals among the faculty. In 2007, the University of Cambridge, in common with many other educational and cultural institutions, marked the bicentenary of the abolition of the slave-trade:

> Some of the Cambridge colleges that helped give birth to Britain's anti-slavery movement will host an array of distinguished speakers this weekend as part of ongoing celebrations to mark the anniversary of slavery's abolition.
>
> Among those giving presentations will be Professor Ruth Simmons, the first African-American woman to head an Ivy League University in the United States, and Mark Malloch-Brown, the deputy secretary-general of the United Nations. Their visits form part of a series of events to mark both the 200th anniversary of abolition in 1807, and the university's special connections with the anti-slavery movement. In the late eighteenth century, Cambridge was home to an influential group of academics, businesspeople, traders and policy-makers, who worked to end the slave trade. As early as 1784, the university's vice chancellor, Peter Peckard, also master of Magdalene College, was speaking out against the lucrative Atlantic slave trade and set an essay competition with the question 'Who has the right to enslave someone against their will?' The winner of that competition, an undergraduate at St. John's College called Thomas Clarkson, then spent seven years lecturing all over the country to fuel public indignation against the slave trade.[15]

Cambridge is understandably proud of Peter Peckard, who appears on Clarkson's hydrographic map as the source of one of the key streams that led to the abolition of the slave-trade. But to what extent is Peckard more representative of late eighteenth-century Cambridge – or Magdalene – than his near predecessor, the pluralist Dr. George Sandby, the master between 1760 and 1774, and chancellor of the diocese of Norwich in 1768, of whom the *Ipswich Journal* reported on 13 May 1758: 'On Tuesday was married the Rev. George Sandby, Rector of Denton in Norfolk, to Miss Acres, an accomplished young lady with a genteel fortune'? Her genteel fortune was derived from slave-ownership in Jamaica. Sandby himself appeared as the signatory of a deed for the lease of Tryall estate and the enslaved people attached to it in Jamaica in 1762. In the 1830s, the couple's son the Revd. George Sandby shared in the compensation paid for the enslaved people on the Tryall estate.

---

[15] <https://www.cam.ac.uk/news/cambridge-marks-200th-anniversary-of-slaverys-abolition> [accessed 1 Aug. 2017].

The financial benefits of slave-ownership could, of course, pass separately from ownership itself. Under the will of Walter Kennedy of Suffolk Street, Charing Cross, Middlesex, which was proved on 20 February 1776, Kennedy left his Tobago property – land and enslaved people – in trust (his trustees included his brother William Kennedy, professor of Greek at the University of Aberdeen), with instructions to sell the estates and pay £10,000 to his wife Ann Catharina Wried with the remainder to support his son Hugh John in his minority and then to be his, with contingent remainder to William Kennedy and their two sisters.

The legacies of slave-ownership span generations. The recent biography of the historian and London School of Economics lecturer and professor R. H. Tawney (1880–1962) characterizes his background as 'a family history based on the careful accretion of wealth and local status from relatively humble origins. Like many entrepreneurial families who came to prominence during the Industrial Revolution, later generations purchased landed estates and were enabled by inheritance to divert from business and commerce to scholarship and the church'. In the course of this discussion, the study identifies Tawney's paternal grandmother, Susannah James Bernard, by name.[16] It does not mention that she was co-heiress of her father Dr. Charles Edward Bernard, who was a slave-owner from a dynasty of Jamaica slave-owners and was himself born in Jamaica and died after the end of slavery, having received compensation for 350 enslaved people. Tawney's connection with slave-ownership might not tell us much about Tawney: but it tells us something important about the way in which British history is constructed if such connections are omitted in a case-study of class-formation in Britain in the eighteenth and nineteenth centuries.

Edward Turner was the first professor of chemistry at University College, appointed in 1827, and author of 'one of the best of all nineteenth-century textbooks of chemistry', *Elements of Chemistry* (1827).[17] 'He was born in Jamaica, of pure English blood, eldest son of a prosperous island proprietor there, in the thriving slavery days of our West Indian colonies', according to a late nineteenth-century memoir that epitomizes the rewriting of the history of British colonial slavery to portray Emancipation as a mistake that ruined the colonies or more specifically ruined the former slave-owners and their families.[18] Five of his siblings – although not Edward Turner himself – shared in the compensation awards for the family's Dunbarton estate, and Turner held a power of attorney in the compensation process for his brother.

[16] L. Goldman, *The Life of R. H. Tawney: Socialism and History* (2013), p. 12.

[17] W. H. Brock, 'Turner, Edward (1796–1837)', in *O.D.N.B.* <https://doi.org/10.1093/ref:odnb/27848> [accessed 23 July 2012].

[18] Sir Robert Christison, *The Life of Sir Robert Christison, Bart.* (Edinburgh, 1885), i. 130–3.

Universities also made, and continue to make, discretionary choices about whom to celebrate with honorary degrees. James Ewing of Strathleven, a major mercantile figure in the formation of modern Glasgow and a slave-owner in Jamaica, was awarded an LL.D by the University of Glasgow in 1835. The slave-owner John Gray (who died *c*.1769) was rector (largely a ceremonial position) of Marischal College, Aberdeen between 1762 and his death, although he lived near London on Richmond Hill. Edward, later Sir Edward, Cust, the M.P. and courtier, was awarded an Hon. D.C.L. from the University of Oxford in 1853. He had married Mary Anne Boode, from a slave-owning family in British Guiana, through whom he became an owner of Greenwich Park estate and the enslaved people on it, leading him to write in 1835 to one of the Commissioners of Slave Compensation from his home at Leasowe Castle: 'Dear Stevenson [*sic*]: how much might I hope to receive? I trust I am not intruding an impertinent request ... I see your Brother in Law at Holkham received one royal duchess with very great splendour'.[19]

Undergraduates as slave-owners

A conventional although not exclusive orientation in contemporary contention over the legacies of the past is conflict between students and authorities. But undergraduates were historically (and in some cases remain) members of the elite society around them, and many slave-owning families sent sons to university in Britain. In the eighteenth and nineteenth centuries in England this meant Oxford and Cambridge, sometimes accompanied by attendance at the Inns of Court. In some cases, there was dynastic continuity as multiple generations attended the same university and often the same college: eleven members of the Beckford family matriculated in Oxford in the century between 1726 and 1828, of whom four were at Balliol and three at Christ Church. In other cases, it appears clear that the family was seeking to cement its next generation in the networks of power and privilege in Britain. Benjamin Amory of St. Kitts, for example, in his will proved in 1819, stated that he wished his son John James Amory to be educated at either Oxford or Cambridge and to have an allowance of £400 p.a. while he was there.[20]

---

[19] Letter from Edward Cust, Leasowe Castle, dated 30 Sept. 1835 (The National Archives, T 71/1610). The addressee was Henry Frederick Stephenson, and the brother-in-law referred to was Thomas William Coke, later earl of Leicester: the two men had married sisters.

[20] In the event, it appears that John James Amory, who on his majority inherited his father's Clay Hill estate with 122 enslaved people in 1825, and later purchased a second estate on St. Kitts, West Farm, with 94 enslaved people attached to it, did not attend either university.

It is not possible at present to quantify the importance of slave-owning families to Oxbridge colleges, because we have not undertaken the systematic analysis possible using the alumni rolls of the two universities. Instead we have recorded where known the slave-owners who had attended either of the institutions. This provides rich anecdotal material and a sketch, possibly misleading, of the minimum scale of slave-ownership among undergraduates. To date we have identified almost 400 slave-owners matriculating at Oxford or Cambridge in the period 1763–1834, with a slight preponderance towards Oxford. One quarter of the identified Oxford slave-owners were at Christ Church and nearly half of the Cambridge slave-owners were at Trinity. These concentrations might suggest priorities for systematic work that would look at the status of the undergraduates (that is, pensioner or commoner versus fellow-commoner) and their contribution of fees to their college (and university), relative to the endowments of the colleges.

In the case of Oxford and Cambridge, it appears that slave-ownership made the undergraduates; in the case of Scotland, it appears that the universities made slave-owners, in the sense that the greater vocational emphasis equipped young male Scots for roles in the slave-economy, especially as doctors but also initially as book-keepers and clerks. Thomas Jarvis, for example, had an M.A. from Glasgow and an M.D. from Edinburgh, moving in 1744 to Leyden before going to Antigua, where he practised and through marriage took ownership of Thibou's estate and the enslaved people on it, later becoming president of His Majesty's Council. Again, there is a need for systematic work on the rolls of the Scottish universities to determine the extent of these connections to slavery.

Conclusion

The concerns raised in this paper are not confined to higher education: they apply *mutatis mutandis* to the public schools of the eighteenth and nineteenth century, where anecdotal material suggests that 'West Indian' pupils formed a meaningful component of the school rolls and slave-owners contributed financial and cultural resources. Llandovery College was founded as the Welsh Educational Institution in 1847 by the former slave-owner Thomas Phillips after his offer to endow a chair in Welsh at St. David's Lampeter was turned down. He endowed closed scholarships at Jesus College, Oxford, for Llandovery pupils and he gave 7,000 books to the school. Dollar Academy was founded by the slave-trader John McNabb, who left money for that purpose on 1802. The Revd. David Laing, who co-founded Queen's College, Harley Street and assisted Miss Buss in the foundation of North London Collegiate (where six Laing Scholarships were funded in his memory in the gift of his widow) was the son of a slave-owner in Jamaica and a trustee of the Mount Lebanus estate. At St. John's Leatherhead, Henry Dawes gave £2,500 for the purchase of the land at Leatherhead in 1867: the Henry Dawes Centre, the school's new classroom block named after the nineteenth-century donor, was opened on 13 October 2010 by H.R.H. the duchess of Gloucester, the school's patron. The slave-owner Anthony Morris Storer left his library as well as his prints collection to Eton College. According to the *O.D.N.B.* entry for Storer, 'the collection [of 2,800 volumes] contains thirty-four incunabula, including three Caxtons and five of the Aldine incunabula. There are numerous first editions of Greek and Latin classics, Italian literature and early English plays. There are 388 quartos of the last, as well as the first three folios of Shakespeare. A recent keeper at Eton called the collection "the crowning glory" of the library'.[21]

Widening the field of analysis for slave-connections for the universities themselves would identify for example those descendants of ancestors engaged in the slave-economy who physically shaped new and old universities, such as Alfred Waterhouse, the architect of Old Quadrangle at Manchester in 1903 (which is contended to have given rise to the concept of the 'red brick' university), the son of another Alfred (1798–1873), a cotton broker and partner in Nicholas Waterhouse & Sons who claimed slave compensation as a creditor of a large estate in British Guiana; or Sir George Gilbert Scott, whose middle name honoured his mother's descent from a slave-owning family on Antigua and their eponymous estate, and who oversaw the later phase of the restoration of the chapel at All Souls. It would take in slave-grown crops other than sugar and coffee, notably tobacco: the Wills building at Bristol is beginning to become the centre of attention on this score. And it would take in the most problematic intellectual legacies of slavery, including the invention of 'race', so central a legacy at University College London through the work of Galton.

More broadly still looms the issue of colonialism as such. Addressing these histories is a daunting prospect, and it is not for me to prescribe what forms the exploration should take or what subsequent steps will be appropriate. But it is not a safe assumption, looking at the U.S., that it can't happen here. If nothing is done in Britain, we will all be overtaken, as we will deserve to be.

---

[21] I. K. R. Archer, 'Storer, Anthony Morris (1746–99)', in *O.D.N.B.* <https://doi.org/10.1093/ref:odnb/26591> [accessed 19 Aug. 2016].

10. Risk and reputation: the London blue plaques scheme[*]

Anna Eavis and Howard Spencer

The London blue plaques scheme has been running for just over 150 years. During this time more than 920 plaques have been installed across London, commemorating historically significant individuals on the buildings in which they lived or worked.

The enduring popularity of the scheme is testament to the strength of the concept at its heart, which – like most good ideas – is a very simple one; it celebrates the connection between a famous or significant person and a place. It was first proposed by the Liberal M.P. William Ewart, a reformer who also campaigned for the public funding of free libraries and the abolition of capital punishment for such minor crimes as cattle stealing. In July 1863 he addressed the house of commons on the subject of London's rich historical associations and suggested a scheme to inscribe 'on those houses in London which have been inhabited by celebrated persons, the names of such persons'.[1]

This suggestion by Ewart – whose name has since been immortalized in two London plaques – was enthusiastically taken up by Henry Cole (another plaque recipient), former chairman of the Society of Arts, who persuaded the Society to launch a scheme to erect what were then referred to as 'memorial tablets', in 1866. The Society of Arts was to be the first of four organizations responsible for the scheme. It was followed by the London County Council (L.C.C.) in 1901, and the Greater London Council (G.L.C.) in 1965, which brought the plaques to the wider area administered by the new council, which included most of Middlesex and parts of Surrey, Kent, Essex and Hertfordshire. On the abolition of the G.L.C. in 1985 the plaques scheme passed to English Heritage, which continues to run it today.

Broadly speaking the aims of the scheme have not changed much over all this time. It is designed to commemorate historically significant individuals

---

[*] This article draws on Emily Cole's introduction to *Lived in London: Blue Plaques and the Stories Behind Them* (2009).

[1] *Hansard*, Parliamentary Debates, clxxii (17 July 1863), col. 986.

A. Eavis and H. Spencer, 'Risk and reputation: the London blue plaques scheme', in *Dethroning historical reputations: universities, museums and the commemoration of benefactors*, ed. J. Pellew and L. Goldman (2018), pp. 107–15.

who have lived or worked in London buildings. Preference has always been given to authentic buildings connected with the figure, and for the last fifty years the survival of such a building has been a pre-condition. This does serve to limit the scope of the scheme and means that some individuals go uncommemorated; however, it chimes with one of the key intentions of the scheme's founders, which is that the plaques would act as an incentive for the preservation of historic buildings. While Ewart's original proposal doubtless owed something to the flourishing civic and national preoccupation with commemoration, which found expression in public monuments of various kinds, his suggested link between a person and a building was something rather different. It not only celebrated individual achievement, but acknowledged the historical significance bestowed upon a building by association. For those interested in – and concerned about safeguarding – London's architectural heritage, the proposed scheme offered the possibility of identifying and helping to protect the city's historic buildings by increasing 'the public estimation for places which have been the abodes of men who have made England what it is'.[2]

From the outset, those awarding the plaques have had to grapple with the question of reputation – both in determining overall historical significance, and in trying to work out whether an apparently worthy individual has any skeletons poised to fall out of the cupboard. The Society of Arts sought to honour individuals 'connected with historical events' and eminent in the fields of arts, manufacture and commerce. The L.C.C. was initially broader in its definition of significance, stating in 1903 that the scheme should celebrate famous Londoners and visitors to London.

The decision about who is, essentially, famous enough has – from the outset – been taken by a committee. The Society of Arts' first committee on 'memorial tablets' numbered among its members Joseph Bazalgette, George Street and Henry Cole and initially worked from lists of candidates prepared by the Society's treasurer George Bartley. In June 1866 it agreed to plaques for Lord Nelson, Sir Joshua Reynolds, Benjamin Franklin and Lord Byron. It also accepted suggestions from donors to the scheme, including the first to a woman – Sarah Siddons – and from the press. The composer Algernon Ashton – a prolific writer of letters to the newspapers – successfully urged the commemoration of figures including John Ruskin, Charles Dickens and Benjamin Disraeli. In 1901 the L.C.C. inherited some of these candidates. Thereafter suggestions came in unsolicited – much as they do today – from private individuals, professional and learned societies, metropolitan borough councils, and representatives of foreign countries. In this organic

---

[2] E. Cole, *Lived in London*, p.5, quoting a statement made by the Society of Arts in 1866.

fashion, the scheme rapidly became an enterprise substantially driven by public suggestions, and this has remained the case. These suggestions were judged in turn by a bewildering number of L.C.C. and G.L.C. committees, including those devoted to the consideration of records and museums, parks and planning. The dedicated Blue Plaques Panel that currently deliberates dates from 1989, and grew out of the London Advisory Committee.

In 1954 the L.C.C. adopted a set of formal selection criteria against which candidates for plaques could be assessed. Their eminence within their own profession or sphere of activity – as judged by their peers – was regarded as a given. It was also seen as preferable that a commemorated figure's name should be recognizable 'to the man of the street of the succeeding generation' – though it was admitted that account needed to be taken of cases where their historical significance was not concomitant with their public profile. Crucially, the new criteria made explicit the necessity for benign and beneficial achievement – commemorated figures should, it was decreed, have made some important and positive contribution to the welfare or happiness of humanity'.[3] The tone might be somewhat Reithian, but this criterion was continued by the G.L.C. after 1965 and, in slightly amended form, is still applied by English Heritage. The assumption of a 'positive contribution' was strongly implicit even prior to 1954 – as may be deduced from the presence of a victor's laurel wreath or garland in the design of the early (from 1903) L.C.C. plaques.

It is undoubtedly more difficult to establish – and, for more recently deceased figures, to predict – lasting significance than it is to record transient fame. Ideas of historical significance evolve over time, and although the perceived importance of some of those commemorated – Mozart, Van Gogh, Gandhi, for example – seems likely to last well beyond our own era, the scheme is bound to reflect the values of each generation responsible for it. In terms of the areas of human endeavour covered, the blue plaque scheme has – right from the outset – shown a clear preference for commemorating figures active in the arts, and in the field of literature in particular. The relative absence of technological innovators and business people was commented on in 1983, when the G.L.C. commemorated a man who was both – Sir Richard Arkwright. More plaques in this vein have followed, but there is still less representation than might be expected for those active in the engine room of Britain's economic development in the eighteenth and nineteenth centuries. Whether this is down to the primacy of the north of England in this development, or is linked to the prejudice against industrialism detected by some scholars (notably Martin Wiener)

[3] Cole, *Lived in London*, p. 16.

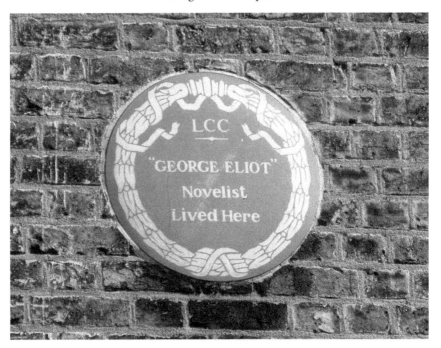

Figure 11.1. George Eliot's L.C.C. plaque of 1905 in Wimbledon Park Road,
Wandsworth, with the wreathed border design. It was the first put up by the
L.C.C. to a woman – and the first official plaque to go south of the River Thames.

among the British elite is a moot point. It could simply be that achievements
in the arts are – for non-specialists – easier to comprehend and therefore
to judge than those in scientific or technological fields. Inevitably, for the
public facing scheme, the bias of the suggestions received plays a part too.

There are – or were – other threadbare patches in the scheme's rich tapestry.
Before 1986 only one sporting great – W. G. Grace – was represented; now,
some two dozen are honoured, from racing car drivers to promoters of the
body beautiful. The first footballers to be commemorated as such – Bobby
Moore and Laurie Cunningham – did not get their plaques until 2016,
a dearth partly explained by the dominance of clubs from the north of
England in the early years of the professional game. But popular culture
in general was given fairly short shrift until the 1960s, when the G.L.C.
put up a slew of plaques to stars of the music hall, including Marie Lloyd,
Dan Leno and – despite considerable dissent on the selection panel, which
was then the G.L.C.'s Historic Buildings Board – Old Mother Riley. More
recently, pop musicians such as Jimi Hendrix, John Lennon and Freddie
Mercury have joined the pantheon of blue roundel recipients.

Figure 11.2. Wilkie Collins was rejected for a blue plaque in 1910 after the clerk of the L.C.C. advised that his writings were 'not of a high order'. His reputation having revived, his rectangular plaque went up in Gloucester Place, Marylebone, in 1951.

Other changes of emphasis over time have affected the number of plaques to women and to figures belonging to minority ethnic groups. It is perhaps unsurprising that only four of the original thirty-five plaques erected by the Society of Arts were for women. More startling is the fact that as early as 1907, this imbalance was perceived as enough of a problem by the L.C.C.'s chief clerk Laurence Gomme for him to write a paper listing some of the notable women who could be commemorated – and some of them were. Even today, the proportion of women commemorated accounts for just 13 per cent of the overall total; this compares with 10 per cent included in the *Oxford Dictionary of National Biography*, as revised in 2004. The first person from an ethnic minority to be commemorated with a blue plaque was Mahatma Gandhi, in 1954; twenty-five years later, just four others had joined him. Under the G.L.C. in the mid 1980s, this rapidly doubled, and subsequent collaboration with the Black and Asian Studies Association helped to take numbers into the twenties. The current total of plaques to black and minority ethnic figures is thirty-four, which accounts for less than 4 per cent of the overall total: efforts to boost the number of nominations in this area are ongoing.

In judging historical significance, there are, of course, questions of degree – John Keats, who was commemorated as long ago as 1896, has undoubtedly maintained his lustre, but how do Arthur Hugh Clough or Raymond Chandler measure up in terms of lasting literary reputation? Both writers were approved in fairly recent years by the Blue Plaques Panel. Careful attention is paid to the composition of the Panel, members of which are selected for their expertise in key subject areas to ensure as broad a view of cases can be taken as is possible. Views are bound to differ on the merits of candidates, but to ensure that – hopefully – wise and informed decisions are made, and that proposals are given the attention they deserve, all suggestions are researched and evaluated by an in-house historian, supported as required by further research commissioned from external historians.

Research has underpinned the scheme since its earliest days, perhaps because of its emphasis on the identification of historic buildings in the changing London landscape. In 1903 the L.C.C. stated that the scheme – in addition to honouring famous Londoners – was designed to provide accurate information about London's history, taken from official records. It became known, until the Second World War, as the Indication of Houses of Historical Interest in London. If the scheme was to contribute to an understanding of London's history, it required investment in research. The L.C.C.'s approach, overseen by the clerk of the council, was meticulous and rigorous, including detailed analyses of rate books and directories, and involving the staff of the council's library division. At times however – usually when resources have been tight – independent research has been skimped on, and the testimony of interested parties apparently accepted without verification. This happened at certain points in the 1980s, for example – a period which saw several instances of poor or even incorrect choices of building for commemoration, and some errors and omissions in plaque inscriptions.

Nor were the 1980s unique in producing plaques with some unfortunate choices of words. In 1931 Sir Francis Galton was celebrated as 'founder of Eugenics' in a private plaque erected by admirers. The plaque was adopted into the official scheme by the L.C.C. in 1959, as was then done on occasion. It is surprising that the council had no qualms about this, as the term eugenics was by that time irredeemably tainted by its association with the racial policies of the Nazis. Galton's plaque may be defended on the basis of his achievements in biostatistics and the advances he made in the study of heredity – but any plaque to him being considered now would – surely – not mention eugenics. An association with or interest in eugenics – once very common – would not, it should be noted, be regarded as a disqualification for a plaque. Several of its one-time devotees have been commemorated for other important achievements, including George Bernard Shaw and Marie Stopes.

The case of Ezra Pound, whose reputation as a poet presently appears unassailable, is more complex. He was first considered for a blue plaque in 1988 by English Heritage, who considered that 'in view of Pound's involvement with Fascism and his support for Hitler and Mussolini, it was too soon to take a dispassionate view of the case for commemoration'. In 1999 it was decided that despite the 'severe stain on his character … his significance as a major poet of the 20th century was sufficient to justify commemoration'. A plaque to Pound duly went up in 2004 at his former home in Kensington Church Walk. The case is illustrative not only of the need for well-informed consideration of evidence, but of the importance of the passage of time arriving at a dispassionate assessment of historical significance. It was a point that was understood from the early years: in 1903 Lord Rosebery, former chairman of the L.C.C., suggested that no plaque

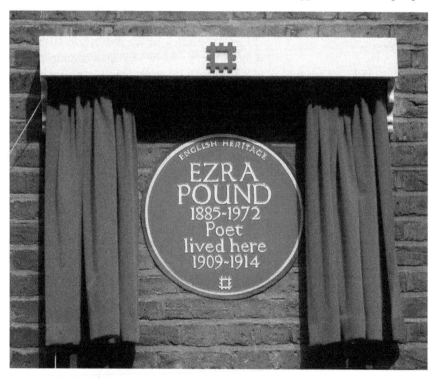

Figure 11.3. The unveiling of Ezra Pound's plaque in Kensington Church Walk took place in 2004.

should be erected for a living person – although his primary concern was apparently to protect the putative living plaque-holder from unwanted public interest. Only one individual – Napoleon III – has ever been given a plaque while still alive – in 1867, while he was still ruling France (the plaque is the oldest to survive). Draft regulations drawn up by the L.C.C. in 1903 proposed that no plaque be installed until twenty-five years after death and from 1912 a 'twenty-year rule' is mentioned in Council papers. In 1947 it was reported that 'it has not generally been the practice to erect a memorial tablet to any person within twenty years of death'. The exceptions included W. E. Gladstone (1908), John Ruskin (1909), T. H. Huxley (1910) and Earl Roberts (1922). In 1954 the 'twenty-year rule' was adopted as part of a formalization of the scheme's procedures by Sir Howard Roberts, clerk to the council. For Roberts this period allowed 'a breathing space in which a man's reputation and achievement can be considered dispassionately'.[4]

For some figures, even twenty years is not enough for a dispassionate and informed judgement to be made. In 2007 English Heritage rejected the case for Wallis Simpson having concluded that that a recent biography's suggestion that she had passed vital information directly to the Nazi and German foreign minister Joachim von Ribbentrop could not be dismissed as merely scurrilous. Additionally, government papers relating to the abdication crisis remain closed until 2036, meaning that vital information is not yet in the public domain. Aside from these considerations it is not entirely clear how Wallis Simpson measures up against the 'positive contribution' clause – and the choice of occupational descriptor for her on a plaque could pose a dilemma too.

This principle of 'wait and see' is a particularly important safeguard against commemorating an individual whose reputation takes a major dive after death. The obvious cautionary example from recent years is Jimmy Savile, whose plaque in Scarborough (erected within weeks of his death by the local civic society) was defaced and then removed as the truth about him emerged over the course of the following year. There are, fortunately, no analogous cases in the London plaque scheme, and it is to be hoped that continued adherence to the twenty-year rule will guard against such mistakes from being made. The downside of the rule – that many of a chosen figure's associates and contemporaries will not be around to enjoy the accolade – is probably a price worth paying.

From 1965 until 2013 it was possible to commemorate candidates 'of exceptional fame and longevity' under the official London scheme if they were deceased and 100 years had passed since birth. In practice this meant

---

[4] Cole, *Lived in London*, p. 16.

the consideration of people who had only died a very few years before. It proved impossible to make an effective and credible judgement on the longevity of their significance, given that insufficient time had passed to allow for the emergence of any significant downsides to their reputation. The 'centenary provision' was thus abandoned when the criteria were revised in 2013, though existing cases that had already been shortlisted were not dropped.

The blue plaques scheme's insistence on (to use the present wording) 'some important positive contribution to human welfare or happiness' has been criticized. It has been asked how certain commemorated individuals can reasonably be reckoned to have crossed that hurdle – and with some, like Hiram Maxim, whose best-known invention was the first fully automatic machine gun, it is not an easy question to answer. More generally, the criterion has been attacked as an archaic hangover from the era of whig history. Such criticism fails to take account of the particular challenges of running the scheme, which is currently financed by charitable donations and has in the past been run on public money: either way, the use of such funds to commemorate the merely notorious would be unlikely to work to the long-term advantage of the plaques scheme. Perhaps an even more practical consideration is that the vast majority of buildings commemorated are in private hands, and the plaques are there by the grace of their owners – another barrier to the celebration of the infamous. This is more than a theoretical possibility. In East London, a building survives that Josef Stalin apparently stayed in as a young man; curiously, no blue plaque suggestion has so far been received. If one were to come in, there would be a solid and immediate reason for refusing it and – whig history or not – that might seem like a prudent idea.

11. 'A dreary record of wickedness': moral judgement in history

Brian Young

Historians, for whatever reason, rarely feature prominently in any list of that curious category the 'public intellectual'. We can all think of exceptions, no doubt, but they are few and far between, and are, I think, diminishing in number. Historians tend to be broadcasters rather than moralists, penny-a-liner journalists rather than secular Jeremiahs. But this was not always so, and in accounting for why many more historians belonged in the long nineteenth century to that capacious category christened by Stefan Collini as 'public moralists' the historian has to do what he or she does best, and that is to think historically.[1] In undertaking such an examination we can also begin to ask why it has taken so long for such a very necessary conference as this to consider the outbreak of moralizing Maoism that lies behind the 'Rhodes Must Fall' campaign and allied activities at Yale University. Fundamentally, we have ceased to think historically as a culture and this has profound consequences of which the attack on our undoubtedly morally dubious (and sometimes more than merely dubious) ancestors is likely to be but the prelude.

It might well be that the era of historicism and its successors, that is roughly from the very late eighteenth century to the late twentieth century, will eventually look like an intellectual interlude and that the hegemony of history as a *cicerone* to the public memory of humanity will prove fleeting. Moralizing is easy, but it is one of Job's comforters; thinking critically and above all historically is much harder, but it is ethically much more rigorous and hence the reluctance of many to undertake it. We need to be careful to see that the false securities of the 'Whig Interpretation of History' do not collapse into the no less delusory 'Prig Interpretation of History', and priggishness and censoriousness lie behind a lot of what we are confronting today. What E. P. Thompson, a genuine public intellectual, memorably identified in *The Making of the English Working Class* as the 'enormous

[1] S. Collini, *Public Moralists: Political Thought and Intellectual Life in Britain, 1850–1930* (Oxford, 1993).

B. Young, '"A dreary record of wickedness": moral judgement in history', in *Dethroning historical reputations: universities, museums and the commemoration of benefactors*, ed. J. Pellew and L. Goldman (2018), pp. 117–24.

condescension of posterity' can be as attributable to his fellow radicals as it certainly was to the political conservatives he lamented as prominently determining historical interpretation in the early 1960s; a properly self-critical historian, Thompson would, I suspect, have been as suspicious of many aspects of the 'Rhodes Must Fall' campaign as any deluded advocate of absurdly late imperial nostalgia, but much more interestingly and creatively.

Thompson's career as historian and public intellectual marks a moment when the hitherto marginalized and culpably forgotten elements of historical enquiry began to enter the mainstream; from the late 1960s onwards, the academy steadily became more politicized, and hence the 'culture wars' of the 1980s and 1990s; but in his assaults on the Althusserian theorizing of Perry Anderson and other prophets of the New Left, Thompson contrastingly argued for the merits of empiricism and the self-critical mediating of experience as the proper preserve of the historian. Not for him the rhetorical revolutions of Parisian Mandarins.[2] In many ways, Thompson, the enthusiast for William Blake and William Morris, was a legatee of the nineteenth-century public moralists at least as much as he was a public intellectual of the second half of the twentieth century. As the best of the British Marxist historians, and in common with the Labour party, Thompson owed, paradoxically perhaps, more to Methodism than to Marx. However residual religion might have been in Thompson's sensibility, remnants of it allowed him to be more charitable to our ancestors (excluding Methodists) than the more theoretically charged high priests of the New Left tended to be. Christianity, after all and however imperfectly, is a religion predicated on charity and the rehabilitation of the sinner; public chastisement in the early Church initiated the journey on the road to repentance by the individual sinner rather than their ready condemnation to perdition: that was in the hands of an altogether higher authority.

While Thompson thundered from the new University of Warwick and after his resignation from 'Warwick University Limited' from the wilds of Worcestershire, John Burrow pondered in the self-consciously radical schools of study at the University of Sussex on nineteenth-century historians and the various moral universes they inhabited. His conclusions bear reflection, rooted as they are in sceptical reflexivity, to use a word of which he would not have approved, practitioner of it though he splendidly was. And what Burrow concluded was that the whig interpretation of history is actually rather more variegated than its condemners had initially suggested, and that it flourished among tories and radicals as well as among liberals. At its worst, it produced Macaulay, whose philistine prejudices were accurately

---

[2] E. P. Thompson, *The Poverty of Theory: an Orrery of Errors* (1978).

speared by Burrow as being 'suburban', and whose experience of India has been critically and judiciously examined recently by Catherine Hall, and with a remarkable lack of charity let alone sympathy by a Jesuit historian, Robert Sullivan: Macaulay would probably not have been surprised by Sullivan's savaging of his life and writings from the perspective offered by a soupy and excessively moralizing form of contemporary Christianity, if he would rightly have been appalled by it.[3] What Hall remembered and Sullivan wilfully forgot were the lessons of historicism. And historicism, as Burrow remarked in his *History of Histories*, was rooted in a religious view of history: Ranke's idiosyncratic variety of Lutheranism informed every aspect of his activity as an historian.[4]

Historicism has had many historians, of whom the most interesting is Friedrich Meinecke, himself an historian compromised by complicity with the Nazi regime that it took him a suspiciously long time to condemn, and this only in the expiring agony of defeat. But even so appalling a trajectory as that more or less willingly followed by this eventual successor to Ranke's chair at the University of Berlin ought not to mean that Meinecke is simply condemned without a hearing or the benefit of a jury. What is more, as has been noted by his more charitable interpreters, in celebrating the moral and religious capaciousness and attentiveness of historicism in the 1930s, Meinecke was championing a mode of thought that implicitly challenged Nazi ideology. Nazis believed in myth, not in history, in centralizing unity and not in pluralistic variety. Burckhardt, in whom in many ways the historicist tradition culminated, was despised by Nazis. They hated Burckhardt's scepticism and his suspicion of linear narratives; multiplicity and variety were the very stuff of history for Burckhardt, and it was from him that Isaiah Berlin took the repeatedly necessary warning against 'the terrible simplifiers' of human experience.[5] Terrible simplifiers have a taste for purging, and it is not only statues that they tend to throw from pedestals. History and its necessary and highly complex variety is loathed by the terrible simplifiers, whose destructive energy is applied to dismiss rather than to comprehend complicated legacies. And to comprehend is not necessarily to forgive; it is simply and entirely to comprehend.

---

[3] J. W. Burrow, *A Liberal Descent: Victorian Historians and the English Past* (Cambridge, 1981); C. Hall, *Macaulay and Son: Architects of Imperial Britain* (2012); R. E. Sullivan, *Macaulay: the Tragedy of Power* (Cambridge, Mass., 2009).

[4] J. W. Burrow, *A History of Histories* (2007), pp. 457–62.

[5] See B. Young, 'Intellectual history and *historismus* in post-war England', in *A Companion to Intellectual History*, ed. R. Whatmore and B. Young (Chichester, 2016), pp. 18–35, and 'History', in *Historicism and the Human Sciences in Victorian Britain*, ed. M. Bevir (Cambridge, 2017), pp. 154–85.

Not that all historicists were so hesitant to condemn as had been Burckhardt. His contemporary Lord Acton was a hanging judge in the court of historical enquiry; a cosmopolitan Catholic where Burckhardt was a religious sceptic, a Gladstonian Liberal where Burckhardt was a sceptical Bernese conservative, Acton was never less than certain in making historical judgements, whereas Burckhardt was judiciously circumspect. The greatest twentieth-century critic of the whig interpretation of history, Herbert Butterfield, once signally devoted considerable interpretative energy to overturning Acton's 'black legend' exegesis of the St. Bartholomew's Day Massacres. There was something of a paradox in a Methodist historian defending the likes of Catherine de Medici from the moralizing scrutiny of a liberal Catholic, but such is the invigorating nature of our subject and the reflectively distancing discipline it demands of us. Butterfield undertook this work as a proponent of what he called 'technical history' against the moralizing certainties of whiggish mythography; it is a bracing enterprise and has much to commend it. In tackling this subject, Butterfield was reversing a critique Acton had offered of another charitable student of Medici history, Mandell Creighton.[6] (And where, incidentally, would Florence be without the Medici? Statues of the Medici have not been toppled in that city since the late fifteenth century, and let us hope that that continues to be the case. As Burckhardt demonstrated in his *Civilisation of the Renaissance in Italy*, the state was itself a work of art and a work of art that commissioned many other works of art to the benefit of humanity, well beyond that city).

Mandell Creighton is a figure that has been forgotten by all too many historians, but his work was at least as important as that of Acton, and unlike Acton, Creighton achieved his relatively short life's work in the five volumes of his *History of the Papacy*. Creighton began this work in a Northumberland rectory, before completing it as Dixie Professor of Ecclesiastical History at Cambridge, where Acton was to become Regius Professor of History. Acton admired Creighton's industry, but he was highly critical of what he thought to be his altogether too forgiving, if not merely indulgent, treatment of the supposedly culpable moral degeneracy of the Renaissance papacy, most especially of its Medici representatives. No-one could accuse Acton of indirection in his lengthy review of Creighton's *History*, where Acton observes of his adversary that, 'He is not striving to prove a case, or burrowing towards a conclusion, but chooses to pass through scenes of raging controversy and passion with a serene curiosity, a suspended judgment, a divided jury, and a pair of white gloves'. And thence, by contrast, to Acton's peroration in this 1887 review-essay:

---

[6] H. Buttterfield, 'Lord Acton and the massacre of St Bartholomew', in *Man on his Past: the Study of the History of Historical Scholarship* (Cambridge, 1955), pp. 171–201.

Mr. Creighton perceives the sunken rock of moral scepticism, and promises that he will not lower the standard of moral judgment. In this transition stage of struggling and straggling ethical science, the familiar tendency to employ mesology in history, to judge a man by his cause and his cause by its result, to obviate criticism by assuming the unity and wholeness of character, to conjure with great names and restore damaged reputations, not only serves to debase the moral standard, but aims at excluding it. And it is the office of historical science to maintain morality as the sole impartial criterion of men and things, and the only one on which honest minds can be made to agree.[7]

Here is the crux of the Acton-Creighton correspondence that inevitably followed such a declaration of war. Two citations from Acton's letter to Creighton of 5 April 1887 are worthy of repetition, even if both are pretty familiar:

Power tends to corrupt and absolute power corrupts absolutely. Great men are almost always bad men, even when they exercise influence and not authority: still more when you superadd the tendency or the certainty of corruption by authority. There is no worse heresy than that the office sanctifies the holder of it. That is the point at which the negation of Catholicism and Liberalism meet and keep high festival, and the end learns to justify the means.

From which he concluded that, 'You would spare the criminals, for some mysterious reason. I would hang them, higher than Haman, for reasons of quite obvious justice; still more, still higher, for the sake of historical science'.[8] Creighton patiently replied to his apparently liberal persecutor in conciliatory tones, but strictly without giving interpretative way. One paragraph in particular stands out, and it ought to be engraved in letters of gold in every teaching manual for historians that might conceivably be imagined:

You judge the whole question of persecution more rigorously than I do. Society is an organism and its laws are an expression of the conditions necessary for its own preservation. When men were hanged in England for sheep stealing it was because people thought that sheep stealing was a crime and ought to be severely put down. We still think it a crime, but we think it can be checked more effectively by less stringent punishments. Nowadays people are not agreed about what heresy is; they do not think it a menace to society; hence they do not ask for its punishment. But the men who conscientiously thought heresy a crime may be accused of an intellectual mistake, not necessarily of

---

[7] Lord Acton, review of Creighton's *History of the Papacy*, in *Essays in the Study and Writing of History: Selected writings of Lord Acton*, ed. J. Rufus Sears (Indianapolis, Ind., 1986), at pp. 367, 373–4.

[8] Acton, *Essays in the Study and Writing of History*, pp. 383–4.

a moral crime. The immediate results of the Reformation were not to favour free thought, and the error of Calvin, who knew that ecclesiastical unity was abolished, was a far greater one than that of Innocent III who struggled to maintain it. I am hopelessly tempted to admit degrees of criminality, otherwise history becomes a dreary record of wickedness.[9]

The applicability of the Acton-Creighton encounter to the subject of this volume is obvious, and it is accordingly worth quoting that final sentence of Creighton's again: 'I am hopelessly tempted to admit degrees of criminality, otherwise history becomes a dreary record of wickedness'. Surely this is the sensible response of any historian, other than an Actonian moralist, to the issues with which we are concerned today. No-one is going seriously to defend the records of Cecil Rhodes or John C. Calhoun, but their degree of criminality has to be understood in context. Of course, they are more akin to Calvin than to Innocent III in Creighton's reckoning in that both Rhodes and Calhoun lived in a world in which criticism of their attitudes and behaviour towards people over whom they claimed racial superiority was readily voiced by their contemporaries. But even here, curiously, double standards apply. So far as I am aware, the debates over 'Rhodes Must Fall' have not been extended to include the man after whom the Trades' Union-sponsored college at Oxford is named. The posthumous reputation of John Ruskin, aside from justified feminist criticism of his failures regarding his estranged wife Effie Gray, is seemingly sacrosanct; and yet he put his name – as did not only Thomas Carlyle but also Charles Dickens, Charles Kingsley and Alfred, Lord Tennyson – to the Governor Eyre Defence Committee. Governor Eyre had put down a revolt in Jamaica with great savagery, as a result of which John Stuart Mill set up the Jamaica Committee to seek his judicial prosecution, an endeavour in which Mill was joined by Charles Darwin, T. H. Huxley and Thomas Hughes.[10] Why, one wonders, has the eponymous hero of Ruskin College not been subjected to the same travails as Rhodes? Where is the moral consistency in such evasiveness? To use Acton's language, white gloves are worn when Ruskin is discussed, but hanging is held as being too good for Rhodes. Any defence of Ruskin, and they ought to be made, is dependent on Creighton's 'degree of criminality' approach to the exercise of moral judgement in history. But so, uncomfortably, is Rhodes. And what applies to Calhoun ought, surely, also to apply to Thomas Jefferson, but who has consistently advocated any complete rejection of its founder by the University of Virginia?

---

[9] Creighton to Acton in *Essays in the Study and Writing of History*, pp. 389–90.
[10] B. Semmel, *The Governor Eyre Controversy* (1962).

Moral absolutes are not the natural ethical register of historians, and they have not been since Gibbon resorted to irony in withholding judgement on the role played by religion in the decline and fall of the Roman empire. One can deduce aspects of his thinking on the matter, but anyone who insists that Gibbon believed that Christianity was the principal causal agent in that history simply cannot have read his work anything like attentively. Moral absolutes are the coinage of such doubtful historians as Carlyle and James Anthony Froude; and not only ought historians to understand and describe the moral lives of their dead subjects historically and sensitively, but they ought also to be able to imagine how their own judgements will one day be duly historicized in their turn. Creighton knew not only how to live in charity with the Renaissance papacy but also with his contemporary believers and unbelievers, both publicly and privately, when he was preferred from Cambridge first to the bishopric of Peterborough and thence to that of London. Historians, as Gibbon reminded us in the opening of chapter fifteen of his great work, are not theologians and have to understand accordingly how religion (and morality) evolved in time, and not *sub specie aeternitatis*. It is a division of labour we historians should never forget, so permit me to remind you of it (and what Gibbon says of religion can and ought to be extended to politics, morality and ethics):

> The theologian may indulge the pleasing task of describing Religion as she descended from Heaven, arrayed in her native purity. A more melancholy duty is imposed on the historian. He must discover the inevitable mixture of error and corruption, which she contracted in a long residence upon earth, among a weak and degenerate race of beings.[11]

Gibbon, who knew his theology and his casuistry, was always wary of the self-righteous and the persecutory elements in history; they were still extant in the eighteenth century, and they are with us now. The secular ideals of political correctness display much of the intolerance and lack of understanding that made so much of the religious history of the West peculiarly unattractive to liberal sensibilities, and they presume a moral superiority that will not withstand scrutiny. To advocate historical scepticism is, to them, to promote a liberal heresy. Humility as well as scepticism characterizes the best historical practice, and just as Gibbon implicitly cites Augustine in that passage just quoted, allow me to close my remarks with a very slight emendation of a great moral admonition as uttered by a well-known moral teacher, the inspiration alike of Acton and of Creighton: 'Let him who is without sin cast the first stone'.

---

[11] E. Gibbon, *History of the Decline and Fall of the Roman Empire,* ed. D. Womersley (3 vols., Harmondsworth, 1994), i. 446.

12. We have been here before: 'Rhodes Must Fall' in historical context

Lawrence Goldman

The I.H.R. conference from which these papers are drawn explored the relationship between philanthropy and ideology in different historical periods and situations. Recent controversies concerning the morality of gifts to educational and cultural institutions, and over the ideas and behaviour of donors, seemed to us to require historical contextualization. It was our hope that historians, curators, fundraisers and heritage professionals, by reaching back to explain aspects of the history of philanthropy, by examining specific gifts in context, and by considering their own practices, would replace the intensely partisan and present-minded arguments of recent times with examples and case-studies based on careful reflection and scholarship.

The *locus classicus* for recent debates over these questions in Britain is the 'Rhodes Must Fall' affair in Oxford during 2015–16 as has been noted by several of the contributors to this collection. For many people, whether engaged in the controversy or just observing it, at issue was the moral and historical reputation of Cecil Rhodes himself. The relationship of the controversy to philanthropy has not attracted as much attention, however. Yet it was reported at the time that many former members of Oriel College were threatening to cease supporting it financially if the statue of Rhodes was removed. This was not an ideological reaction on their part: there was no hint that anyone endorsed Rhodes's behaviour and views more than a century later. Rather, it represented a concern that if the college could dishonour a benefactor and his benefactions in this manner, under pressure from students articulating the ideas of the present, it might treat their donations to the college, given in good faith, in the same manner at some future date. These also might be judged outmoded or tainted, and reassigned to another purpose or even given back.[1]

---

[1] 'Cecil Rhodes statue to remain at Oxford University after alumni threaten to withdraw millions', *The Daily Telegraph*, 29 Jan. 2016 <http://www.telegraph.co.uk/education/universityeducation/12128151/Cecil-Rhodes-statue-to-remain-at-Oxford-University-after-alumni-threatens-to-withdraw-millions.html> [accessed 18 Apr. 2018]

L. Goldman, 'We have been here before: "Rhodes Must Fall" in historical context', in *Dethroning historical reputations: universities, museums and the commemoration of benefactors*, ed. J. Pellew and L. Goldman (2018), pp. 125–38.

Opposition to monuments, statues and commemorations from the past which are held to offend people today is thus intimately linked to the act of giving: most of these offending memorials have been given to universities, colleges and museums by donors, or have been set up to remember benefactors or illustrious public figures and paid for by subscription. To pull them down is not only to dispute the historical legacy of the subject but to take issue with those who supported the memorial. It is also to take issue with an earlier interpretation of the past, one that we may no longer agree with. But is disagreement or even the taking of offence a strong enough reason to remove a monument or alter a benefaction that a past generation endorsed and celebrated?

We have been here before, though past controversies over educational benefactions have not been ideological in the same way. The Victorians were nothing if not hard-headed and empirical, and their disputes were over *the use* of donations and the social benefit thereby derived from them, rather than the beliefs of the donor. Nevertheless, they provide an interesting context for understanding our present disputes.[2]

The 1850s and 1860s were an era of educational investigation and reform in Britain at all levels as the fragmented and inadequate provision of schools and colleges was addressed by commissions of enquiry and legislation. Secondary education was of dubious quality in schools which were unregulated and unexamined, and middle-class parents were (as they always are about education) disgruntled and unhappy. I have no doubt that mid Victorian dinner parties were, as now, consumed with the discussion of the merits of the local schools. Eventually, after years of debate and much hand-wringing over national failure, Palmerston's government established a royal commission in 1864 to examine the state of secondary education, the Taunton Commission.[3] This reported in 1868 after an exhaustive and exemplary review of educational provision and recommended that existing educational endowments – funds donated and invested over the centuries for educational purposes – should be reapplied to support high-quality secondary education. At this stage, there was no state funding for secondary

---

[2] The following discussion of the reform of endowments for secondary education in mid-Victorian Britain is taken from my essay 'The defection of the middle classes: the Liberal Party and the 1869 Endowed Schools Act', in *The Political Culture of Victorian Britain: Essays in Memory of Colin Matthew*, ed. P. Ghosh and L. Goldman (Oxford, 2006), pp. 118–35. See also L. Goldman, *Science, Reform and Politics in Victorian Britain: the Social Science Association 1857–1886* (Cambridge, 2002), pp. 236–61.

[3] *Royal Commission to Inquire into Education in Schools in England and Wales* (known as the Schools' Inquiry or Taunton Commission), 21 vols. (Parl. Papers 1867–8, xxviii), pts. i–xvii.

education: the aim was to reorganize the use of those historic funds given for education by benefactors in the past.

Most of the funds were benefactions dating back to the sixteenth and seventeenth centuries for local boys' grammar schools, providing for the education of all the local boys, whatever their backgrounds. However, over time, many of these benefactions had lost their rationale. Some country schools had enormous sums for the education of a handful of boys; other parts of the new urban and industrial economy had no access to endowments at all. And the educational reformers of the 1860s were generally opposed to providing a free education to the children of the poor using historic funds – they favoured reapplying the money to high quality secondary education of the middle class.

A year after the Taunton Commission report, the new Liberal administration, Gladstone's first government, passed the 1869 Endowed Schools Act. This established the remarkable Endowed Schools Commission (E.S.C.) and charged it with the wholesale reform of these educational endowments, leaving it free to do what it liked, more or less. The E.S.C. had only three members: Gladstone's brother-in-law, Lord Lyttelton, with whom the prime minister corresponded in classical Greek;[4] Arthur Hobhouse, a leading barrister;[5] and Canon Hugh Robinson who had been principal of a teacher-training college in the York diocese. It was said that the E.S.C. could 'take the endowments from a boys' school in Northumberland and apply them to create a girls' school in Cornwall'. Certainly, it behaved in very radical ways by transferring endowments wholesale to create what it hoped would be efficient and high-calibre schools by using historic funds more effectively. Note, by the way, that reference to a girls' school in Cornwall, because the E.S.C. has a very distinguished record in supporting girls' secondary education and in founding several leading girls' schools of today.

Contemporaries saw it differently, however. They were aghast at the unrestrained radicalism of the E.S.C. which seemed to represent the worst aspects of Liberal reform – of Mr. Gladstone in a hurry. It was an embodiment of the trend towards centralization which many Victorian men of property opposed. Local boards of governors were astonished when dictated to by this central body constructed by Liberal legislation which was now overruling local elites used to running these charities themselves.

---

[4] P. Gordon, 'Lyttelton, George William, fourth Baron Lyttelton and fourth Baron Westcote (1817–1876)', in *O.D.N.B.* <https://doi.org/10.1093/ref:odnb/17307> [accessed 17 Oct. 2017].

[5] C. E. A. Bedwell, 'Hobhouse, Arthur, Baron Hobhouse (1819–1904)', rev. H. C. G. Matthew, in *O.D.N.B.* <https://doi.org/10.1093/ref:odnb/33902> [accessed 17 Oct. 2017].

The cry went up of 'local self-government'. In another manifestation of its Liberalism, the Commission regularly asked for evidence that the schools it was reforming were Anglican in origin and practice, which had hitherto been taken for granted. Indeed, in the historical literature on the Endowed Schools Act, it is this religious difficulty which is usually held to have led to the most controversy. In reality, the Commission's treatment of traditional and inefficient governing bodies which were brushed aside as the E.S.C. took away endowments, and which in some cases effectively closed down long-standing local schools, was the real cause of conflict.

The Commission caused controversy wherever it went, but especially when it turned to the reform of the Emanuel Hospital Foundation in Westminster in 1871. In that year the foundation was educating sixty-four boys on an income of over £2,000 per annum. The E.S.C. believed it could do better and put forward a plan, involving amalgamation with three other foundations, to create three new boys' schools and use the endowments to educate fully 900 boys. The scheme would also have removed the court of aldermen of the City of London as the governing body – in other words, the E.S.C. was on a collision course with men of property from the City of London and there could be only one winner. It led to a public meeting at the Mansion House in April 1871 to protest against the scheme and more generally to oppose and rein-in the E.S.C.. Simultaneously, these issues were taken up in parliament by among others, Lord Salisbury, later the Conservative prime minister. He pointed out the effects of such interference on the act of giving itself, the same point made by Oriel College's alumni in 2015–16. If donors, he argued, could not be certain that their gifts 'will not be devoted to some philosophical crotchet of the day there will be no more bequests or endowments'.[6]

There were many reasons why the Liberals lost the 1874 general election but among them was the reaction to the Endowed Schools Act which was the subject of much protest, many letters to local and national newspapers, and many critical editorials in those newspapers. In London alone in 1874 it is estimated that the issue helped to swing seven seats away from the Liberals, and across England as a whole it seems to have been one of those defining issues which alienated the middle class from the party they had hitherto supported, leading many of them to abstain or vote Conservative. In short, the reform of Victorian educational endowments had genuinely important political consequences.

---

[6] For Salisbury's speech in parliament, see Hansard, *Parliamentary Debates*, ccv (24 Apr. 1871), cols. 1549–58; ccvii (30 June 1871), cols. 862–9 (Goldman, 'The defection of the middle classes', p. 131).

The surprising result of all this controversy was that one of the first things the Conservatives did on forming a government after the 1874 election was effectively to repeal the 1869 legislation in the Endowed Schools Amendment Act. I say surprising, because, according to Gladstone himself, this was the first ever case of legislation being repealed on partisan lines in all of British history, and he may well have been correct. While we are used to the repeal of legislation by an incoming government, up to the 1870s governments tended to respect what had gone before and leave it alone. Under the amending act, the responsibilities of the E.S.C. were handed over to the far more cautious and conservative Charity Commission. There was another result, as well: the suicide of Lyttelton in 1876.

This whole saga may appear at first sight to be about local powers, the threat of centralization and the wounded *amour propre* of Victorian men of property who sat as school governors. But it was also a profoundly philosophical contest concerning the relations of past and present. Interestingly, these mid Victorians did not seem worried over the provenance of the endowments, or the moral record of those who donated the funds, whether from mad bad kings, exploitative local landholders, or ill-gotten from the dissolution of the monasteries. But they did worry over what was known as 'the dead hand', as if stretching from the grave and trying to maintain control of endowments according to the benefactor's intentions, even in altered circumstances centuries later. This was the position of the liberal radicals: that the 'dead hand' should be cut off. On the other side, however, were organic conservative thinkers who venerated an unbroken link between past and present. For example, the Revd. Dr. William Irons, prebendary of St. Paul's Cathedral, vicar of Brompton, and the author in 1869 of a work entitled *The Analysis of Human Responsibility*, said in that year:

> If they were to cut themselves off, and say they had nothing to do with the past, and nothing to do with posterity, they would only intensify the selfishness of the present generation, and threaten the progress of all civilization. It should never be forgotten that they owed all they had to their forefathers, and were morally bound to transmit all the advantages they could to those who came after them.

The reform of educational endowments in the mid Victorian period was a much bigger and more politically significant question than 'Rhodes Must Fall'. It was not just about the way our views of the past change over time – indeed, it wasn't much about that at all – but concerned the way the material and financial inheritance we receive from our ancestors is treated, whether respectfully or radically. But in this respect, it is not unlike the controversy over Cecil Rhodes and the threat that it poses to the act of giving: the alumni of Oriel College now, and the corporation of London then, share a similar aversion to meddling with their philanthropy.

What, then, should we do about monuments, buildings, scholarships, even names that are found to be offensive because of an association with a belief or practice now out of favour or even condemned? The problem is not confined to British imperialists, of course, but has been burning at a much higher intensity in the United States over relics of the Confederacy, the history of African-American slavery, and the denial of black civil rights after slavery was abolished by the Thirteenth Amendment to the U.S. constitution in 1865. At an earlier seminar at the I.H.R. (October 2016) two different responses were suggested. Professor Martin Daunton, the economic and social historian, spoke in favour of contextualizing monuments by siting biographical detail and historical information close by, so as to explain how views of past deeds and reputations have changed over time. Professor David Starkey, on the other hand, argued that nothing should be done to alter the historic fabric and that any sort of apology for what are now considered misdeeds or crimes could have neither force nor validity as coming from generations and people who were not responsible. His argument was to leave the material inheritance of the past as we have found it, but to ensure that historians rigorously pursue the truth of past actions and beliefs without a hint of sentiment and without any desire to excuse.[7] It is not unlike the position taken by Nicholas Draper in this collection of essays (see chapter 9) who argues here that when questions are raised about institutional associations with slavery (and by extension any great moral wrong), the institution concerned should, at the very least, have done its homework so that it can be open and honest about its degree of responsibility and culpability. If a college or school or church has undertaken due diligence, it will have shown the requisite moral courage, and demonstrated that it takes the matter seriously.

Other solutions include re-siting offensive monuments in sculpture parks for the outmoded and unadmired. Tiffany Jenkins has drawn attention to Delhi's Coronation Park in her essay in this collection.[8] Another such place exists in Moscow, the Muzeon Sculpture Park on the banks of the Moskva River, about a mile from Red Square, where all the unloved and unlamented statuary and relics of Bolshevism and the Soviet Union have been collected together.[9] It is a favourite spot for a romantic stroll with a partner, apparently

---

[7] *History Now and Then* seminar: 'Rhodes' statue and beyond', held at the Institute of Historical Research, 5 Oct. 2016. The other speakers were Professors Margot Finn and Jinty Nelson.

[8] See p. 86 above.

[9] 'Russia's statues solution: a sculpture park', *The Chicago Tribune* <http://digitaledition.

– a contemporary Russian take on 'love among the ruins', the title of a poem by Browning, of a painting by Burne-Jones, and of several more recent novels, films and plays as well. But to do this is to decontextualize the monuments and obstruct historical understanding: where a statue is erected, its juxtaposition to other buildings and monuments, its relationship to civic space in general, is a crucial element of its historic significance and intrinsic to the understanding of its purpose. In any case, as responsible authorities like Historic England made clear during the 'Rhodes Must Fall' affair, permission to alter the historic fabric in such a manner would not be granted.[10] There is also the suggestion that while doing no violence or injustice to existing monuments, the problem can be addressed by erecting statues to, and otherwise commemorating, those whom we now respect and admire in order to redress the ideological balance. This might be the least controversial solution, though the very politicization of public monuments in recent years will make the commissioning of public statuary a more difficult process now and in the future.[11] A consensus may be as elusive over the identity of those nominated to receive public recognition in the present and future as it has been when considering celebrated figures from the past. And there is always the danger that the 'other side' in these debates, whatever their ideological stripe, will have their revenge in time, and turn on today's heroes just as yesterday's have been dethroned and removed.

Another response when the controversy is caused by the very identity of the figure being remembered and honoured is a change of name. The renaming of Calhoun College by Yale University has been noted by several of our essayists. That the University authorities decided first in 2016 to retain the name of Calhoun College, but then changed their minds a year later is evidence of the degree of difficulty in breaking with the past and of the new force of student activism in these questions. When explaining the original decision made in 2016 to retain the given name, Yale's president Peter Salovey wrote that: 'retaining the name forces us to learn anew and confront one of the most disturbing aspects of Yale's and our nation's past. I

---

chicagotribune.com/infinity/article_popover_share.aspx?guid=a1e6c04a-7a80-4254-97a6-a76i0198ec91> [accessed 18 Apr. 2018].

[10] 'Removal of Rhodes statue "could be blocked due to its historical interest"', *The Daily Telegraph*, 19 Dec. 2015 <http://www.telegraph.co.uk/education/educationnews/12059379/Removal-of-Rhodes-statue-could-be-blocked-due-to-its-historical-interest.html> [accessed 18 Apr. 2018].

[11] This suggestion was made by Professor Eric Foner of Columbia University at a public seminar in the British Library, 9 Jun. 2017, on 'The use and abuse of American history. Eric Foner in conversation with Lawrence Goldman'. See also 'A usable past: an interview', in E. Foner, *Battles for Freedom: the Use and Abuse of American History. Essays from The Nation* (New York, 2017), p. 213.

believe this is our obligation as an educational institution'.[12] Name changing may antagonize alumni and possibly alter the behaviour of present and future benefactors for reasons already discussed. But as Salovey's comment also suggests, its unintended result is to expunge from the record not only tainted names but also the knowledge of former actions, beliefs and their consequences.

The same points have been made in relation to the planned renaming in this country of Bristol's famous Colston Hall, announced in April 2017, and the wider campaign to have the name of Colston removed from every building, monument, street and scholarship in the city.[13] Edward Colston was a slave trader of the late seventeenth and early eighteenth centuries and a major benefactor of Bristol who provided for schools, almshouses and a bridge. Now, in the words of one opponent of the campaign, 'he is to be airbrushed out of history'.[14] Alumni of Colston's Girls' School in the city also demurred on learning that Colston's name would not be mentioned at an annual commemoration of benefactors' service in Bristol Cathedral: 'do not attempt to ignore the historic past, however unsavoury' was their response.[15] 'History should not be obscured' wrote another opponent.[16] Once the name has been removed and, in this case, Colston has become a

---

[12] I. S. Becker, 'Yale keeps the Calhoun name despite racial concerns, but ditches the "Master" title', *The Washington Post*, 27 Apr. 2016 <https://www.washingtonpost.com/news/grade-point/wp/2016/04/27/yale-keeps-the-calhoun-name-despite-racial-concerns-but-ditches-the-master-title/?utm_term=.8eb69b271de2> [accessed 18 Apr. 2018].

[13] 'Bristol's Colston Hall to drop name of slave trader after protests', *The Guardian*, 26 Apr. 2017 <https://www.theguardian.com/uk-news/2017/apr/26/bristol-colston-hall-to-drop-name-of-slave-trader-after-protests> [accessed 18 Apr. 2018]; 'Historic Bristol music venue Colston Hall ditches name shared with "toxic" slave trader. Could the Colston bun be next?', *The Daily Telegraph*, 26 Apr. 2017 <http://www.telegraph.co.uk/news/2017/04/26/historic-music-venue-colston-hall-ditches-name-shared-toxic/> [accessed 18 Apr. 2018].

[14] K. Morgan, 'Colston, Edward (1636–1721)', in *O.D.N.B.* <https://doi.org/10.1093/ref:odnb/5996> [accessed 16 Oct. 2017].

[15] 'Slave trader Edward Colston cut out of school service in his honour', *The Daily Telegraph*, 19 Oct. 2017 <http://www.telegraph.co.uk/news/2017/10/19/slave-trader-edward-colston-cut-school-service-honour/> [accessed 18 Apr. 2018]; letters from Paula and Gillian Gardner and Jonnie Bradshaw. *The Daily Telegraph*, 24 Oct. 2017.

[16] Letter, J. Harratt, *The Daily Telegraph*, 6 Nov. 2017 <http://www.telegraph.co.uk/opinion/2017/11/06/lettersrights-accused-must-not-fall-victim-latest-moral-panic/> [accessed 18 Apr. 2018]. At the time of writing it looks as if the alumni have been successful as the headteacher has confirmed that the school will not be changing its name (see 'Headteacher of school founded by slave trader Edward Colston says he refuses to "obscure history" by changing its name' <http://www.telegraph.co.uk/education/2017/11/02/headteacher-school-founded-slavetrader-edward-colston-says-refuses/> [accessed 18 Apr. 2018]). However, at the end of 2017 it was announced that after extensive consultations, Colston *Primary* School was removing 'Colston' from its name.

Figure 12.1. Statue of Edward Colston by the sculptor Edward Cassidy, erected in The Centre, Bristol, in 1895, and the 'unauthorised heritage' plaque affixed to its base which remembers the millions of victims of the Atlantic slave trade.

remote and forgotten figure, it will be more difficult to engage critically with Bristol's central role in the history of the Atlantic slave trade. In Oxford, the Codrington Library, in its name alone, opens up many ways of thinking about the past. Remove the name and call it just the All Souls Library and the complex legacy of a wealthy slave-holding dynasty in the West Indies, and the relationship between the profits of slavery and philanthropy, are that much more difficult to recover and discuss.[17] While buildings and benefactions carry the names of their donors or their inspirations, it is an easy task to find out their failings and learn from them, or to be transported back to another age and way of thinking. Imagine the loss to Manchester and the nation if we were to change the name of the Free Trade Hall, that monument to a great idea situated in the city that campaigned so ardently in the 1830s and 1840s for a new *laissez-faire* political economy? Expunge the name and not only has the past been distorted; identities will have ceased to have any educative function.

Thus far, the discussion has focused on the objects of complaint, the monuments, statues and buildings representing a past that, in the views of some, must be confronted. But how do we explain the change in attitude, especially among students, which has made this such an issue in recent years? In the United States, it may be a reflection of a return to the exercise of power by student groups which was a feature of American higher education and wider politics in the 1960s and 1970s. American commentators have also pointed to a profound decline in respect for traditional liberal values like free speech and free expression on American campuses.[18] It may also be linked to the increasingly partisan nature of American life in general. Entrenched blocs of the left and right can find no common ground and even seem unwilling to seek it. In the politicization of all things, even statues to long-dead and long-forgotten figures may become controversial.

In the United Kingdom, there may be another reason as well, one that bears on the role and responsibility of historians and teachers: the nature of the history curriculum itself. For understandable reasons, the syllabus has tried over the past three decades to focus on key events and passages in modern history from which it is hoped that pupils might learn lessons

---

[17] S. Mandelbrote, 'Codrington, Christopher (1668–1710)', in *O.D.N.B.* <https://doi.org/10.1093/ref:odnb/5795> [accessed 16 Oct. 2017]; '"Take it down!": Rhodes Must Fall campaign marches through Oxford', *The Guardian*, 9 March 2016 <https://www.theguardian.com/education/2016/mar/09/take-it-down-rhodes-must-fall-campaign-marches-through-oxford> [accessed 18 Apr. 2018]; <https://www.asc.ox.ac.uk/library-history> [accessed 18 Ap. 2018].

[18] A. Sullivan, 'A Point of View: The battle for free speech', *B.B.C. Radio 4*, 15 Oct. 2017, <http://www.bbc.co.uk/programmes/b097ck09> [accessed 18 Apr. 2018].

that apply to life in a liberal, democratic and multicultural society. This has led to an increased focus on aberrant and extreme regimes in recent history such as Nazi Germany, Fascist Italy and the Soviet Union under Stalin. Though representations by historians and even by the German ambassador to examination boards, and discussion of the issue in the media, have led to a widening in the choice of subject for public examination, these are still the bedrock of many G.C.S.E. and A-level syllabuses. Students in the United Kingdom studying history for the International Baccalaureate have also specialized in recent years in the specific study of 'dictators', from Hitler and Mussolini to Mao and Castro. It is also now common to meet students studying the history of American civil rights and South African apartheid as core components of the A-level course.

There can be little doubt of the interest and moral engagement with these and other subjects like them. But whether students have studied the worst in human nature or the best, whether they have focused on the history of persecuting regimes or the struggle of subject peoples to be free, they have been presented with history as a morality play, a struggle between unmistakeable good and evil. In the process, they will have learnt much about basic democratic rights and the need to protect liberal values and constitutional arrangements, which must be to the good. These courses will have helped prepare them for citizenship, for sure. But whether they will have gained a subtle and reflective view of the past is questionable. History, focused on these subjects, is more likely to be understood as a sequence of Manichean struggles in which right and wrong are so clear as to need little discussion. The habits thus learned in the class and lecture room, largely based on a narrow range of modern historical examples, may be too easily applied to other situations where the context is more complicated and 'the sides' less clear.

It is rare indeed to find students who have studied the distant past for its own sake: medieval history has almost disappeared at A-level and even the Tudors seem to be in decline. The imaginative engagement with the 'differentness' of the past has been displaced by a history chosen and designed to be relevant today. This is not to accuse anyone involved of bad faith but it is to wonder if, in the desire to use the curriculum to convey other social messages, we have encouraged the teaching of 'bad history' by exposing students to a limited range of periods and subjects designed to evoke strong moral responses. To teach periods and themes which are different, even alien to the students of today – medieval kingship, the Reformation, the civil wars of the seventeenth century, Victorian politics – might encourage that more nuanced response to the past which is more accepting of its difference and which is not so swift to judge.

The complexity, diversity and sheer 'difference' of the past has been captured in one of the major new historical resources of the present generation, the *Oxford Dictionary of National Biography* (*O.D.N.B.*), which may provide us with a concluding example of the manner in which present-mindedness can be reconciled with history. No publication is more concerned with biographical detail and the assessment of public lives than the *O.D.N.B.*, the record of more than 60,000 Britons, widely defined as such, over two millennia, who achieved notability in their various fields. At more than 70 million words, it is the longest work in the history of the language. Published online since 2004, it is possible to alter any aspect of a biographical essay as new evidence comes to light or as public attitudes change.

To give a relevant example of updating, some of the findings of the 'Legacies of British Slave-ownership' project at University College, London, whose members include Dr. Nicholas Draper, have been integrated into the *O.D.N.B.* since the publication of their research in 2013.[19] The *O.D.N.B.* was largely written between 1992 and 2004, long before their research project started and the information they have so expertly unearthed about British slaveholding became available. Notwithstanding their criticisms of the *O.D.N.B.* in 2014 and subsequently for its omission of information on slaveholding, and Dr. Draper's examples from the *O.D.N.B.* in his essay in this collection,[20] with Dr. Draper's help in 2016 the Dictionary published thirty-five new biographies of slaveholders in British colonies and recipients of compensation who owned slaves at the time slavery ended in the British empire in 1833, and linked 140 existing Dictionary entries to the Legacies of British Slave-ownership website so that details of their holdings and dealings were easily accessible.[21] Four of the slaveholders with entries

---

[19] *Emancipation and the Remaking of the British Imperial World*, ed. C. Hall, N. Draper and K. McClelland (Manchester, 2014); *Legacies of British Slave-Ownership: Colonial Slavery and the Formation of Victorian Britain*, ed. C. Hall *et al.* (Cambridge, 2016).

[20] *Emancipation and the Remaking of the British Imperial World*, ed. C. Hall *et al.*, pp. 1–2.

[21] A full account of what was done and a listing of new lives added to the *O.D.N.B.* can be found at <http://www.oxforddnb.com/page/september-2016-update#slave_ownership> [accessed 18 Apr. 2018]. Related points may be made about my biography of R. H. Tawney which is mentioned by Dr. Draper on p. 103 above. The research for that book was conducted up to 2011 and the book published in 2013, the same year that the database of the Legacies of British Slaveholding project went live. Like very many scholars and historians, I did not have the benefit of the admirable research of the 'Legacies' project which has established the extent of the slaveholdings of Tawney's maternal great-grandfather. But as I wrote somewhat earlier following publication of the *O.D.N.B.*, 'That one scholar knows more than another is not a cause for complaint but the motor of academic progress'. See 'The Oxford Dictionary of National Biography and the structures of contemporary knowledge', *Times Literary Supplement*, 3 Feb. 2005, pp. 4–5. There is no

in the *O.D.N.B.* mentioned by Dr. Draper in his essay – Joseph Brooks Yates, Thomas Phillips, Edward Turner and Anthony Morris Storer – are linked in this way. As further information is made available by the project, which is now investigating British slaveholding in earlier periods, it can be integrated in, and linked to the *O.D.N.B.* That could not be the case with its predecessor, the original paper and print *Dictionary of National Biography* (*D.N.B.*), begun in 1882 and edited first by the Victorian intellectual, Leslie Stephen. For all its many merits – and it was still being used extensively until 2004 – many of the *D.N.B.*'s essays, and all those concerning major historic figures, were outdated long before it was superseded.

Yet the new dictionary was not written to be 'our view' of national history – the view taken by scholars writing in the twelve years when the *O.D.N.B.* was compiled, and subsequently. To have written it in this way would have limited its usefulness and ensured that it, too, would have become outmoded relatively quickly. Colin Matthew, the *O.D.N.B.*'s architect and first editor, wanted the new Dictionary to build on the first.[22] Thus, no historical figure with an entry in the original *D.N.B.* was cast out, however insignificant and uninfluential they seem now. Articles on lesser figures about whom not much more was known or could be added, were revised rather than researched and written afresh. And the *O.D.N.B.* website was designed to provide instant online access to the digitized version of the first *D.N.B.*, making it possible to work simultaneously from the two versions, comparing and contrasting views from the 1990s with those of the 1890s. Matthew was conscious and desirous of producing a hybrid, an organic and evolutionary work by design, that built on the original *D.N.B.* and which followed its example of publishing well-written, informative and signed rather than anonymous essays about past figures.[23] Previous scholarship was not discarded or ignored but conserved. When Matthew initially sought the views of historians on how to rewrite the dictionary he sent them essays from the original *D.N.B.* and asked for their comments on how they could be improved and developed. Many articles in the *O.D.N.B.* end with a review of the reputation of the subject precisely because in this way we can appreciate changing interpretations and fashion, and balance between past and present views.

---

evidence from the Tawney archives at the L.S.E., other family papers, or other biographies, that R. H. Tawney was even aware of his great-grandfather's slaveholdings; the family wealth, such as it was, came also from boat-building, provincial banking, brewing and purely local enterprise in the 18th century.

[22] R. McKibbin, 'Matthew, (Henry) Colin Gray (1941–1999)', in *O.D.N.B.* <https://doi.org/10.1093/ref:odnb/73078> [accessed 20 Oct. 2017].

[23] H. C. G. Matthew, *Leslie Stephen and the New Dictionary of National Biography* (Leslie Stephen Lecture, 1995) (Cambridge, 1996).

Figure 12.2. Statue of Oliver Cromwell outside the house of commons, Westminster, designed by Hamo Thornycroft and erected in 1899.

This may be the reason for the *O.D.N.B.*'s success as a preeminent source and tool for research – that it was planned as a synthesis of views, old and new, respectful of its inheritance though never flinching from contemporary judgement. Matthew told contributors to be 'wise, liberal and just', not iconoclastic and revisionist for their own sake. Of course, it is easier to deal with changing historical interpretations in print than it is when those interpretations are captured once and for all time in oils, or stone, or in a photograph. The depth and subtlety so obtained in an extensible work of replaceable words, and at such length, is impossible to achieve in mute images, representations and objects which thereby incite more extreme responses. But the hybrid nature of the *O.D.N.B.*, the balance that it has found between past and present interpretations, gives some indication of the spirit required in other areas of public life. Commemoration and memorialization must reflect history and biography as understood *then* as well as now. We should respect and keep faith with the views of previous generations even when, as will so often be the case, we now think differently.

In April 2018, a new statue was unveiled in Parliament Square, Westminster.[24] It depicts the great champion of women's suffrage from the 1860s to the 1920s, the leader of the National Union of Women's Suffrage Societies, Millicent Garrett Fawcett.[25] It is entirely uncontroversial; indeed, if there is an issue at all, it is why it has taken so long to honour her in this manner and why she will be only the first woman memorialized in Parliament Square.[26] Across the road from Dame Millicent, however, just within the precincts of the Palace of Westminster, is an imposing statue of Oliver Cromwell, sword and bible in his hands and lion at his feet, with a much more complex history. Cromwell sat in the house of commons as M.P. for Cambridge from 1640 and he led parliament's forces in the Civil War. But he also signed Charles I's death warrant; put to death Leveller mutineers in the New Model Army; benefited from Colonel Thomas Pride's purge of conservative members of the house of commons in December 1648, a manoeuvre in which he may well have been involved; invaded and subdued Ireland while massacring some of its population; and ruled alone without a parliament as Lord Protector in the 1650s.[27] It is hardly surprising that the suggestion by the Liberal government of Lord Rosebery in 1895 that a statue be erected in his honour should have met with public and parliamentary disfavour and a subsequent decision by the government to withhold funding.[28] But an anonymous donor paid for the statue out of his own pocket and it was eventually unveiled in 1899, when it was discovered that the donor was the now former prime minister, Rosebery himself.[29] Controversial then, as recently as 2004 a motion in the house of commons from a group of M.P.s led by the late Tony Banks, called for the statue to be removed and melted down.[30] But Cromwell still bestrides Westminster, evidence perhaps of the maturity and reflectiveness of British and also Irish political culture. As this essay has tried to show, whether or not Rhodes should or will fall, we have been here before.

---

[24] Live interview with the author on the occasion of the statue's unveiling, *B.B.C. Radio Suffolk*, 24 Apr. 2018 <https://www.bbc.co.uk/programmes/p0633xgp> [accessed 25 Apr. 2018].

[25] J. Howarth, 'Fawcett, Dame Millicent Garrett (1847–1929)', in *O.D.N.B.* <https://doi.org/10.1093/ref:odnb/33096> [accessed 17 Oct. 2017].

[26] 'Artist unveils design for Parliament Square suffragist statue', *The Guardian*, 20 Sept. 2017 <https://www.theguardian.com/artanddesign/2017/sep/20/artist-gillian-wearing-unveils-design-parliament-square-statue-suffragist-leader-millicent-fawcett> [accessed 18 Apr. 2018].

[27] J. Morrill, 'Cromwell, Oliver (1599–1658)', in *O.D.N.B.* <https://doi.org/10.1093/ref:odnb/6765> [accessed 17 Oct. 2017].

[28] *The Times*, 20 Apr., 15 Jun., 18 Jun. 1895.

[29] *The Times*, 26 Apr., 2 May, 23 Sept. 1899.

[30] 'Oliver Cromwell statue moving', *News of the World*, 16 May 2004, p. 29.

Bibliography

Albrecht, H., *Alfred Beit: the Hamburg Diamond King* (Hamburg, 2007, Eng. trans. 2012)

Ashby, E. and M. Anderson, *Portrait of Haldane at Work on Education* (1974)

Barkan, E., *The Guilt of Nations: Restitution and Negotiating Historical Injustices* (Baltimore, Md., 2001)

Barnado, S. L. and J. Marchant, *Memoirs of the late Dr. Barnardo* (1907)

Bevir, M. (ed.), *Historicism and the Human Sciences in Victorian Britain* (Cambridge, 2017)

Biggar, N. (ed.), *Burying the Past: Making Peace and Doing Justice After Civil Conflict* (Georgetown, D.C., 2003)

Bowden, M., *Pitt Rivers: the Life and Archaeological Works of Lieutenant-General Augustus Henry Lane Fox Pitt Rivers, DCL, FRS, FSA* (Cambridge, 1991)

Brent, R., *Liberal Anglican Politics: Whiggery, Religion and Reform 1830–1841* (Oxford, 1987)

Brock, M. G. and M. C. Curthoys (eds.), *The History of the University of Oxford, vii: Nineteenth-Century Oxford, part 2* (Oxford, 2000)

Brown, P., *Through the Eye of a Needle: Wealth, the Fall of Rome and the Making of Christianity in the West, 350–550 AD* (Princeton, N.J., 2012)

Brown, W. *States of Injury: Power and Freedom in Late Modernity* (Princeton, N.J., 1995)

Burrow, J. W., *A Liberal Descent: Victorian historians and the English Past* (Cambridge, 1981)

— *A History of Histories* (2007)

Butterfield, H., *Man on his Past: the Study of the History of Historical Scholarship* (Cambridge, 1955)

Cannadine, D., *The Decline and Fall of the British Aristocracy* (New Haven, Conn., 1990)

Charlton, H. B., *Portrait of a University 1851–1951: to Commemorate the Centenary of Manchester University* (Manchester, 1951)

Christison, R., *The Life of Sir Robert Christison, Bart.* (Edinburgh, 1885)

Cole, E., *Lived in London: Blue Plaques and the Stories Behind Them* (Yale, 2009)

Collini, S., *Public Moralists: Political Thought and Intellectual Life in Britain, 1850–1930* (Oxford, 1993)

Crossman, R. H. S., *The Role of the Volunteer in the Modern Social Service* (Sidney Ball Memorial Lecture, 1973)

Daunton, M., *Trusting Leviathan: the Politics of Taxation in Britain, 1799–1914* (Cambridge, 2007)

Draper, N., *The Price of Emancipation* (Cambridge, 2010)

Emden, P. H., *Jews of Britain: a Series of Biographies* (1944)

Fabian, J., *Time and Other: How Anthropology makes its Objects* (New York, 1983)

Fiddes, E., *Chapters in the History of Owens College and of Manchester University 1851–1914* (Manchester, 1937)

Foner, E., *Battles for Freedom: the Use and Abuse of American History. Essays from the Nation.* (New York, 2017)

Gay, H., *History of Imperial College London 1907–2007: Higher Education and Research in Science, Technology and Medicine* (2007)

Ghosh, P. and L. Goldman (eds.), *Politics and Culture in Victorian Britain: Essays in Memory of Colin Matthews* (Oxford, 2006)

Gibbon, E., *History of the Decline and Fall of the Roman Empire* (ed. D. Womersley, 3 vols., Harmondsworth, 1994)

Goldman, L., *Science, Reform and Politics in Victorian Britain: the Social Science Association 1857–1886* (Cambridge, 2002)

— *The Life of R. H. Tawney: Socialism and History* (2013)

Hall, A. R., *Science for Industry: a Short History of the Imperial College of Science and Technology* (1982)

Hall, C., *Macaulay and Son: Architects of Imperial Britain* (2012)

Hall, C., N. Draper and K. McClelland (eds.), *Emancipation and the Remaking of the British Imperial World* (Manchester, 2014)

Bibliography

Hilton, B., *A Mad, Bad, and Dangerous People? England 1783–1846* (Oxford, 2006)

Hobson, J. A., *The War in South Africa* (1900)

— *Imperialism: a Study* (1902)

Hopkins, C., *Trinity: 450 Years of an Oxford College Community* (Oxford, 2005)

Jenkins, T., *Keeping their Marbles: How the Treasures of the Past Ended Up in Museums – and Why They Should Stay There* (Oxford, 2016)

Lonetree, A., *Decolonizing Museums: Representing Native America in National and Tribal Museums* (Chapel Hill, N.C., 2012)

Lowenthal, D., *The Past is a Foreign Country* (Cambridge, 1985)

— *The Heritage Crusade and the Spoils of History* (Cambridge, 1998)

McKenna, J., *British Ships in the Confederate Navy* (Jefferson, N.C., 2010)

MacKenzie, N. and J. MacKenzie (eds.), *The Diary of Beatrice Webb*, ii: *1892–1905* (1983 ed, Cambridge, Mass.)

Mack Smith, D., *Cavour and Garibaldi 1860: a Study in Political Conflict* (Cambridge, 1954)

Mignolo, W. D., *The Darker Side of Western Modernity* (Durham, 2011)

Muir, R., *Plea for a Liverpool University* (Liverpool, 1901)

Murch, J., *Memoir of Robert Hibbert, Founder of the Hibbert Trust: with a Sketch of its History* (Bath, 1874)

O'Hanlon, H. M., *The Pitt Rivers Museum: a World Within* (London and Oxford, 2014)

Owen, D., *English Philanthropy 1660–1960* (Cambridge, Mass., 1965)

Peers, P., *Shrunken Heads* (Oxford, 2011)

Rotberg, R. L., *The Founder: Cecil Rhodes and the Pursuit of Power* (Oxford, 1998)

Rubin, M., *The Hollow Crown* (2005)

Ruston, A. R., *The Hibbert Trust: a History* (1984)

Sears, J. R. (ed.), *Essays in the Study and Writing of History: Selected writings of Lord Acton* (Indianapolis, Ind., 1986)

Semmel, B., *The Governor Eyre Controversy* (1962)

Shinn, C. H., *Paying the Piper: the Development of the University Grants Committee 1919–46* (Falmer, 1986)

Simon, N., *The Art of Relevance* (Santa Cruz, Calif., 2016)

Smith, L. T., *Decolonizing Methodologies: Research and Indigenous Peoples* (1999)

Sullivan, R. E., *Macaulay: the Tragedy of Power* (Cambridge, Mass., 2009)

Thomas, K. V., *The Ends of Life: Roads to Fulfilment in Early Modern Britain* (Oxford, 2009)

Thompson, E. P., *The Poverty of Theory: an Orrery of Errors* (1978)

Torpey, J. (ed.), *Politics and the Past: on Repairing Historical Injustices* (Lanham, Md., 2003)

Torpey, J. *Making Whole What Has Been Smashed: on Reparations Politics* (Cambridge, Mass., 2006)

Trevelyan, R., *Grand Dukes and Diamonds: the Wernhers of Luton Hoo* (1991)

Vernon, K., *Universities and the State in England 1850–1939* (Abingdon, 2004)

Waddilove, L. E., *Private Philanthropy and Public Welfare: the Joseph Rowntree Memorial Trust 1954–1979* (1983)

Webb, S., *London Education* (1904)

Wellmon, C., *Organizing Enlightenment: Information Overload and the Invention of the Modern Research University* (Baltimore, Md., 2015)

West, R. W., *All Roads are Good: Native Voices on Life and Culture* (Washington, D.C., 1994)

Whatmore, R. and B. Young (eds.), *A Companion to Intellectual History* (Chichester, 2016)

Wheatcroft, G., *The Randlords: the Men Who Made South Africa* (1985)

Whyte, W., *Redbrick: a Social and Architectural History of Britain's Civic Universities* (Oxford, 2015)

Williams, E., *Capitalism and Slavery* (Chapel Hill, N.C., 1994 [1944])

Wilson, D. and D. Sperber, *Meaning and Relevance* (Cambridge, 2012)

Index

A-level history syllabus, 135

Aberdeen, University of, 95, 100, 103

Acton, John Emerich Edward Dalberg, first baron, 120–3

Aikenhead, John Lawrence, 101

All Souls College, Oxford, 18, 23, 73, 95, 99, 106, 134

Americans, native, 21–2, 83

Amory, Benjamin, 104

Amory, John James, 104

Anderson, Perry, 118

Anglo-Confederate Trading Co., 99

Anthony Nolan Trust, 58

Antigua, 105, 106

Arkwright, Sir Richard (blue plaque), 109

Arts Council, 47

Ashmolean Museum, Oxford, 21

Ashton, Algernon, 108

Association of Leading Visitor Attractions (A.L.V.A.), 70

Atkins, John, 96

Audi, Alan, 90

Audley, Sir Thomas, 18

Augustine of Hippo, 47, 51, 55, 123

Balfour, Arthur James, first earl of Balfour, 36, 41

Balliol College, Oxford, 18, 27, 104

Balliol, John de, 18

Banks, Tony, 139

Barbados, slavery and slaveholding in, 73, 96

Barkan, Elazar, 92, 93, 98

Barnardo, Dr. Thomas, 61

Bartley, George, 108

Bass, Lee, 3

Bazalgette, Joseph, 108

Beaufort, Lady Margaret, 15, 17

Beckford, family of slaveholders in Jamaica, 104

Beit, Alfred, 35, 37–46

Beit, Otto, 38, 40, 42–3, 45

Belloc, Hilaire, 45

Benin bronzes, 22, 77, 81–2, 84, 91

Berlin, Isaiah, 119

Berlin, University of, 47, 52, 119

Bernard, Susannah James, 103

Bernard, Charles Edward, 103

Bessemer Laboratory, Royal School of Mines, 46

Bessemer memorial fund, 40

Beyer, Charles, 29–30

Birmingham, University of, 1, 2, 29, 30, 34, 58

Black and Asian Studies Association, 111

'Bloody Sunday' massacre (Londonderry, 1972), 83

Bodleian Library, Oxford, 15

Bodley, Sir Thomas, 1, 15

Boer War, 23, 39, 45

Bogue, Tony, 93

Bolton, John, 96

Boode, Mary Anne, 104

Bristol, Colston benefactions to, 132–4

Bristol, University of, 1, 2, 24, 27, 29–30, 106

    opposition to the Wills' benefactions, 31n, 106

British Guiana, 96, 104, 106

British South Africa Company, 5, 39

Brooklyn Museum, 74

Brown, Gordon, 58

Brown University, vii, 34, 94

Brunel University, 34

Brunner, John, 30
Burckhardt, Jacob, 119–20
Burns, John, 45
Burrow, John, 118
Butterfield, Herbert, 120

Calhoun, John C., 6–7, 9, 122
Calhoun College, Yale University, 6–7,
    93n, 131–2
Cambridge, city of, 139
Cambridge, University of, 1, 15–18,
    26–7, 33, 47–55, 81–2, 84, 95,
    102, 104–5, 120, 123
    Advisory Committee on
    Benefactions and External Legal
    Engagements (A.C.B.E.L.A), 50–55
    benefactions to, 49–55
Cambridge Assessment, 49
Cambridge University Press, 49
Cameron, David, 61, 83
Cape Town, University of, vii, 5–7, 42
    origins of 'Rhodes Must Fall'
    movement at, 85
Cardiff Metropolitan University, 32
Carlyle, Thomas, 122–3
Carnegie, Andrew, 2, 40
Carnegie Trust, 61
Cavendish Laboratory, University of
    Cambridge, 1
Central Lancashire, University of, 32
Central Mining and Investment
    Corporation Ltd., 43
Chadwick, Owen, 12
Chamberlain, Joseph, 2, 58
Chandler, Raymond (blue plaque), 112
Charlottenburg, Technische
    Hochschule, 36
Christ Church, Oxford, 17, 18, 104,
    105
Christie, Richard Copley, 29
Christ's College, Cambridge, 17, 18
City and Guilds Institute, 36, 41–2
City Parochial Charities Act 1883, 28

City University, 34
Clarkson, Thomas, 102
Clifton College, 27
Clothworkers' Company, 27
Clough, Arthur Hugh (blue plaque),
    112
Codrington, Christopher, 23, 73
Codrington estates, Barbados, 96
Codrington Library, Oxford, 73, 95,
    99, 134
Cole, Sir Henry, 107–8
Collini, Stefan, 117
Collins, William Wilkie (blue plaque),
    111
Colston, Edward, 132–3
    Colston Hall, 132,
    Colston Girls' School, 132
    Colston Primary School, 132n
commemoration of benefactors,
    ceremonies for, 1
Common Ground, 74
Cook, Captain James, voyages of, 77
Cornell, Ezra, 34
Coronation Park, Delhi, 86, 130
Creighton, Mandell, 120–3
Crewe, Robert Offley Ashburton
    Crewe-Milnes, first marquess of
    Crewe, 45
Cromwell, Oliver, 139
    statue of in Westminster, 138–9
Crossman, R. H. S. (Richard), 58
Cunningham, Laurie (blue plaque),
    110
Curzon, George, first marquess Curzon
    of Kedleston, 28
Cust, Sir Edward, 104

Darwin, Charles, 68, 122
Daunton, Martin, 130
Davies, Howard, 3
Davis, Jefferson, 85
Dawes, Henry, 106
Dawkins, John, 99

Dawkins, Richard, 99
De Beers Consolidated Mines, 38, 42
decolonization, 85–6
De-colonial Cultural Front (U.S.), 74
Decolonize the Museum Critical
    Communities' Collective
    (Netherlands), 73–4
Denver Museum of Nature and
    Science, 22
Devonshire, Spencer Comton
    Cavendish, eighth duke of, 41
Dickens, Charles, 108, 122
Dictionary of National Biography, 137
Disraeli, Benjamin (blue plaque), 108
Dolby, family gift to the University of
    Cambridge, 49
Dollar Academy, 105
Draper's Company, 28
Dudley, John William Ward, first earl
    of, 96
Duffy, Eamon, 24
Duke, James Buchanan, 34
Dunbarton estate, Jamaica, 103
Durham Cathedral, 27
Durham, University of, 27

Edinburgh, University of, 95, 105
educational endowments, Victorian
    reform of, 25–8, 126–30
Edward VII, 36, 40, 42
Edward Lawrence & Co., 99
Eliot, George (Mary Anne Evans) (blue
    plaque), 110
Elshtain, Jean Bethke, 88
Elgin marbles, the, 90–1
Emanuel Hospital Foundation, 128
Emory University, 34
Endowed Schools Act, 1869, 126–9
Endowed Schools Commission, 1869–
    74, 126–9
English Heritage, 107, 114, 131
Eton College, 97, 106
Ewart, William, 107

Ewing, James, 104
Exeter College, Oxford, 17
Eyre, Governor of Jamaica, see
    Governor Eyre Defence Committee

Fawcett, Dame Millicent Garrett, statue
    of, 139
Firth College, Sheffield, 34
Fitzwilliam Museum, Cambridge, 1
Flick, Gert-Rudolph, 3, 20
Foner, Eric, 131n
Franklin, Benjamin (blue plaque), 108
free speech, decline of respect for, 134
Free Trade Hall, Manchester, 134
Froude, J. A., 123

Gaddafi, Colonel, 3
Galton, Francis (blue plaque) 112
Gandhi, Mahatma (blue plaque), 111
George Eliot, see Eliot, George
George Mason University, 34
George Washington University, 34
Georgetown University, vii, 93, 101
Gibbon, Edward, 8, 123
Gladstone family, and slavery, 98
Gladstone, John, 96
Gladstone, W. E. G., 114, 127, 129
Glasgow, University of, 95, 105
Goldsmith's Company, 28
Goldsmith's University of London, 28
Gomme, Laurence, 111
Governor Eyre Defence Committee,
    122
Grace, W. G. (blue plaque), 110
Gray, Effie, 122
Gray, John, 104
Greater London Council (G.L.C.), 107
Great Exhibition, 1851, 36–7
Greenwich Hospital, 101
Greenwich Park estate, British Guiana,
    104

Haberdashers' Company, 28
Haldane, R. B., 35–7, 40–1
Hall, Catherine, 119
Harcourt, Sir William, 45
Harvard, John, 34
Hearing Dogs for Deaf People, 61
Hendrix, Jimi (blue plaque), 110
Heriot-Watt University, 33
Heywood & Co., 98
Hibbert, Robert, 99
Hibbert Trust, 99
Higher Education Act, 2017, 47
Higher Education Funding Council for
    England (H.E.F.C.E.), 47
Hillsborough tragedy (1989), 83
historicism, 117–20
Historic England, see English Heritage
history curriculum, schools', 134–6
Hobhouse, Arthur, first baron
    Hobhouse, 127
Hobsbawm, Eric, 8
Hobson, J. A., 45
Holt, George snr., 99
Holt, George jnr., 99
Hopkins, Johns, 34
Hopper, Grace Brewster Murray, 6
Hughes, Thomas, 122
Humboldt, Alexander von, 47, 52
Huxley, Thomas Henry, 114, 122

Imperial College of Science and
    Technology, vii, 5, 35–7, 40–6, 81
Institute of Historical Research,
    University of London, vii, 2, 4, 125,
    130
Irons, Revd Dr. William, 129

Jamaica, slavery and slaveholding in,
    96, 99–104, 106
    Eyre Rebellion in, 122
Jameson, Dr. Starr, 39
Jameson Raid, 5, 39, 45
Jarvis, Dr. Thomas, 105

Jefferson, Thomas, 85, 122
Jesus College, Cambridge, 81–2
Jesus College, Oxford, 105
John Moores University, Liverpool, 15,
    32
John Rylands Library, Manchester,
    29–30

Keats, John (blue plaque), 112
Keble, John, 26–7
Kellogg College, Oxford, 58
Kennedy, Walter, 103
Kennedy, William, 103
Keogh, Sir Alfred, 45
Kerr, Clark, 25
King's College, Cambridge, 17
King's College, London, 95
Kwoba, Brian, 73

Labouchere, Henry, 45
Laing, Rev. David, 106
Lane Fox, General Augustus, 68–9
Langworthy, Edward, 32
Lawrence, Sir Edward, 99
Leeds Beckett University, 32
Leeds, University of, 1, 27–8, 29
Legacies of British Slave-ownership
    project, 94–5, 136–7
Leicester Polytechnic, 34
Lennon, John (blue plaque) 110
Leno, Dan (blue plaque), 110
Leporius, priest in the fifth century
    church, 51
Leslie, Hugh Fraser, 100
Liverpool, connections with slavery, 96,
    98–9
Liverpool Literary and Philosophical
    Society, 98
Liverpool Royal Institution, 98
Liverpool, University of, 1, 24, 29–30,
    58, 97–8
Llandovery College, 105
Lloyd, Marie (blue plaque), 110

Lobenguala, king of the Matabele, 5
London County Council (L.C.C.) 37, 40–1, 107–14
London School of Economics, 3, 10, 36n, 103, 137n
London, University of, vii, 1, 27, 35–6
Louis Napoleon, see Napoleon III
'Love Among the Ruins' (Browning, Burne-Jones et al), 131
Lyttelton, George William, fourth baron Lyttelton, 127–9

Macaulay, T. B., 118–9
Mack Smith, Denis, 24
McNabb, John, 105
Magdalen College, Oxford, 18
Magdalene College, Cambridge, 18
Malik, Kenan, 86
Manchester, 19
Manchester Mechanics Institute, 33
Manchester, University of, 1, 24, 29–30, 32, 34, 106
Manning, William, 96
Manning & Anderdon, West India merchants, 96–7
Markland, James Heywood, 101
Mason, Josiah, 30
Mason College, Birmingham, 30
Matthew, Colin, 137
Maxim, Hiram (blue plaque), 115
Maxwele, Chumani, 85
Medical Research Council (M.R.C.), 57
Meinecke, Freidrich, 119
Mellon, Andrew, 4
memorial museums, 84
Mercury, Freddie (blue plaque), 110
Mill, John Stuart, 122
Montford, P. R., 43–4
Moore, Robert ('Bobby') (blue plaque), 110
Moores, John, 15
morality, history and, 120–3, 134–6

Morant, Sir Robert, 41
Mount Lebanus estate, Jamaica, 106
Mowat, Sir Francis, 41
Musée du Quai Branly, Paris, 74
Museum of Fine Arts, Boston, 74
Museums Victoria, Melbourne, Aus., 89
Muzeon Sculpture Park, Moscow, 130

Napoleon III (blue plaque), 114
National Union of Women's Suffrage Societies, 139
Natural History Museum, London, 84
Nazism, historiography of, 119
Nelson, Horatio Lord (blue plaque), 108
Neville, George William, 81
New College, Oxford, 17, 27
North London Collegiate School, 106
Nuffield College, Oxford, 58
Nuffield Foundation, 60

Okukor, the, see Benin Bronzes
'Old Mother Riley' (Arthur Lucan) (blue plaque), 110
Oriel College, Oxford, vii, 5, 6, 15, 84–5, 125, 128, 130
Owens College, Manchester, 29, 34
Owens, John, 29, 30–32
Oxford Dictionary of National Biography, 136–8
Oxford High Street, 5, 84
Oxford Movement, 26–7
Oxford, University of, vii, 1, 3, 5–7, 10, 15–20, 22, 23, 26–8, 33, 47, 58, 59n, 68–9, 73, 74, 76–8, 84–5, 95, 101, 104–5, 122, 125, 134
Clarendon Laboratory, 28
Radcliffe Science Library, 28
Social anthropology department, 28

Pallmer, Charles Nicholas, 96
Peckard, Peter, 102

Percival, John, 27
Petre, William, 17
Petrie, Flinders, 68
Phillips, Thomas, 100, 137
Phillpotts, Rev. Henry, 96
Pitt Rivers, General, see Lane Fox, General Augustus
Pitt Rivers Museum, Oxford, 22, 65–79
  Shuar and Ashuar cultures, 71–2
  tsantas (shrunken heads) in, 22, 71
Pope, Thomas, 18
Pollard, A. F., 2
Porgès, Théodore, 37
Porgès, Jules, 38
Porter, Henry, 90
Pound, Ezra (blue plaque), 113
Power, John Cecil, 2
present-mindedness, 8, 91, 125, 135–7
Princeton University, 3, 6–7, 10
Purdue, John, 34

Queen's College, Harley Street, London, 106
Queen's College, Oxford, 101
Queen Mary University of London, 28
Qwabe, Ntokozo, 85

Randlords, 37, 39, 40, 45
Rathbone, William, 58
Regent Street Polytechnic, 28
reparations (for historic wrongs), 82–3, 86–90
repatriation (of historic artefacts), 22, 75, 81–4, 86, 88–9
restitution (of appropriated artefacts), 82–3, 88–90
Reynolds, Sir Joshua (blue plaque), 108
Rhode Island University, vii
Rhodes, Cecil, vii, 3, 5, 10, 15, 32, 38, 44, 84–6, 122, 125, 139

Rhodes Must Fall (campaign), vii, 5, 6, 19n, 31n, 35, 73–4, 85–6, 117–8, 122, 125, 129, 131, 134n
Rhodes Scholarships, 5, 6, 10, 85
Rhodes University, 42
Robbins Report (Report of the Committee on Higher Education 1963), 2
Robert Gordon University, 33, 58
Roberts, Frederick Sleigh, first earl Roberts (blue plaque), 114
Robertson, Charles, 3
Robinson, Canon Hugh, 127
Rosebery, Archibald Philip Primrose, fifth earl of Rosebery, 36, 40–41, 113, 139
Royal College of Science (R.C.S.), 36–7
Royal School of Mines (R.S.M.), 35–7, 40–1, 43, 45–6
Ruskin, John, 108, 122
Rutgers University, 34
Rylands, John and Enriqueta, 29–30

St. Andrews, University of, 95
St. Catherine's College, Cambridge, 18
St. David's, Lampeter, see University of Wales Trinity St. David
St. John's College, Cambridge, 15
St. John's College, Oxford, 17
St. John's School, Leatherhead, 106
St. Kitts (West Indies), 101, 104
St. Vincent (West Indies), 100
Salisbury, Robert Gascoyne-Cecil, third marquess of, 128
Salovey, Peter, 131
Sandby, Revd George snr., 102
Sandby, Revd George jnr., 102
Sanger Institute, 57
Savile, Jimmy, 114
Scott, George Gilbert, 106

sculpture
    commissioning of, 131
    re-siting of, 86, 130–1
Shaw, George Bernard (blue plaque),
    113
Sheffield, University of, 1, 29, 34
Shirley, Dame Stephanie, 59
Siddons, Sarah (blue plaque), 108
Simmons, Ruth, 93, 102
Simon de Montfort University, 34
Simpson, Wallis, 114
slave trade, Atlantic, 23, 31, 91, 94,
    96–98, 102, 105, 132–4
slavery, v, 6, 19, 23–5, 45, 54, 58, 73,
    84, 91, 93–106, 130, 132–4, 136–7
    abolition in the United States by the
    13th Amendment, 130
    and Quakers, 31
    and universities, 30–1, 93–106,
    contemporary disputes over in the
    United States, 130, 134
Smith, Payne & Smith, bankers, 96–7
Smuts, Jan Christian, 53
Society for the Propagation of the
    Gospel in Foreign Parts, 96, 101
Society of Arts, 107
Spencer, Herbert, 68
Stalin, Josef (blue plaque?), 115
Stanford, Leland, 34
Stanley, Alice, 68
Starkey, David, 130
Stephen, Leslie, 137
Stirling Castle estate, Jamaica, 101
Stopes, Marie (blue plaque), 113
Storer, Anthony Morris, 106, 137
Street, George, 108
Sullivan, Robert, 119
Sussex, University of, 118

Tate family, 31
Tate, Sir Henry, 32, 97

Taunton Commission (Royal
    Commission to Inquire into
    Schools in England and Wales,
    1864–8), 126–7
Tawney, R. H., 103, 136–7n
Tennyson, Alfred, Lord, 122
Thibou's estate, Antigua, 105
Thomas, Keith, 59
Thompson, E. P., 117–8
Thompson, S. A., see S. A. Thompson
    Yates
Thompson, Samuel Henry, 97–8
Tobago (West Indies), 103
Torpey, John, 86–7
Trinity College, Oxford, 18, 101
Trinity College, Cambridge, 105
Tryall estate, Jamaica, 102
Turner, Edward, 103, 137

universities, names of, 32–4
University College, London, 40, 95,
    103, 106, 136
University College London Hospital,
    58
university extension movement, 27
University of Manchester Institute
    of Science and Technology
    (U.M.I.S.T.), 32
University of Wales Trinity St. David,
    100

Vanderbilt, Cornelius, 34
VärldskulturMuseum (Gothenburg), 75
victimhood, growth of, 89–90
Vincent, John, 8
Virginia, University of, 122

Warburg Institute, University of
    London, 2
Warner, Marina, 88
Warwick, University of, 118

Waterhouse, Alfred, 106
Waterhouse, Nicholas & Sons, 106
Weatherall Institute, Oxford, 57
Webb, Aston, 43, 46
Webb, Sidney, Lord Passfield, 35, 40, 41
Wernher, Julius, 35, 37–46
Wernher, Beit & Co., 38, 40–1, 43
West India Planters and Merchants,
    Society of, 96, 101
whig interpretation of History, 117–20
White, Sir Thomas, 17
Whitworth Hall, University of
    Manchester, 29
Whitworth, Joseph, 29–30
Wiener, Martin, 109
Wilberforce, William, 96
William of Wykeham, 17
Williams, Joanna, 82
Willis, Elizabeth, 89
Wills family (Bristol), 2, 30–2, 106

Wilson, Rev. John, 101
Wilson, Woodrow, 3, 6–7
Wilson College, Princeton University,
    6–7
Wried, Ann Catharina, 103
Wolfson College, Oxford, 58
Wolfson Foundation, 4, 57n, 59, 62
Wolsey, Cardinal, 18
Woodrow Wilson School of Public
    Affairs, Princeton University, 3, 6–7
Woolf, Harry, Lord Woolf, 3

Yale, Elihu, 34
Yale University, 3, 6–7, 10, 93, 117,
    131–2
Yates, Elizabeth, 97–8
Yates, Joseph Brooks, 97–8, 137
Yates, S. A. Thompson, 97–8
Youth Business Trust (Prince of
    Wales's), 59

INSTITUTE OF HISTORICAL RESEARCH | SCHOOL OF ADVANCED STUDY UNIVERSITY OF LONDON

The Institute of Historical Research (I.H.R.) is the U.K.'s national centre for history. Founded in 1921, the Institute facilitates and promotes innovative research via its primary collections library, and its programme of training, publishing, conferences, seminars and fellowships. The I.H.R. is one of the nine humanities research institutes of the School of Advanced Study at the University of London.

'I.H.R. Shorts' is a new Open Access publishing series from the Institute of Historical Research at the University of London. Insightful and concise, I.H.R. Shorts offer incisive commentaries on contemporary historical debates. Titles range from 15,000 to 50,000 words with a focus on interdisciplinary approaches to the past.

1. Dethroning historical reputations: universities, museums and the commemoration of benefactors
   edited by Jill Pellew and Lawrence Goldman (2018)

2. Magna Carta: history, context and influence
   edited by Lawrence Goldman (2018)

CPSIA information can be obtained
at www.ICGtesting.com
Printed in the USA
JSHW022226211219
3115JS00001B/8